Front cover Artwork ©RuT

Renowned Artist, Riëtte Delport created the beautiful cover for Sacred Hearts Rising when she heard about the Anthology and the topics of the stories the women would be sharing.

As with the stories within these pages, her art work speaks volumes about women and their everyday challenges placed in their paths.

Thank you, Riëtte, for seeing the true beauty of Sacred Hearts Rising in your exquisite work of art.

See the Supporters Section at the back of the book for more about ©RuT and what she does.

SACRED HEARTS RISING

Breaking The Silence
One Story at a Time

Compiled by Brenda Hammon

Note to the reader: This book is not intended to dispense psychological or therapeutic advice. The information is provided for educational and inspirational purposes only. In the event, you use any of the information in this book for yourself, which is your constitutional right, the author and publisher assumes no responsibility for your actions. Although the Author(s) and Publisher has made every effort to ensure that the information in this book was correct at press time, the Author(s) and Publisher does not assume and hereby declaims any liability to any party for any loss, damage, or disruption by errors or omission, whether such error and omission result from negligence, accidents or any other cause.

Disclaimer: For personal reasons, some of the authors in their chapters have changed names, relationships and locations to protect privacy. These changes have not altered the events themselves.

Other books by Brenda Hammon

Coming Soon 2018 Echoes
The Ripple Effect
Breaking the Cycle Series Book 3 of 3

I AM
Kicking Down the Walls of Silence
Breaking the Cycle Series Book 2 of 3

Hear Me
No Longer Silent
Breaking the Cycle Series Book 1 of 3

I Can't Hear the Birds Anymore
By Brenda Portwood

Table of Contents

"Darkness cannot drive out darkness; only light can do that."

Acknowledgments

What can I say about the amazing women who opted to jump on my 'dream train' of breaking the silence on topics that no one particularly wants to talk about openly and honestly?

All of you are truly inspirational and have added so much to my life and the lives of those that read your story. You have changed the world of so many who are still suffering in silence, and you have given another woman a fighting chance at creating her change in her life.

I have been so honored to have had this opportunity to witness your bravery, and have watched each of you grow while sharing your heartfelt journey.

Riëtte Delport, a thousand thank you's for offering me the use of your amazing artwork for the cover. I am humbled.

To Jen Violi for all your dedication and focus on helping the women tell their inspiring stories.

To Jo Dibblee who bravely accepted the challenge of writing the foreword for this amazing book. A difficult task with so many different stories but you found the common thread amongst us all.

To Colleen Songs who said "Yes," to writing a poem for all of the women who shared their stories, and for writing the "Sacred Hearts" poem about the journey all of the women embarked on. Each poem showed, through beauty and grace, a new way to see their stories.

To Bud; the man who has stood beside me through thick and thin and never wavering, you give me strength when I need it and then stand back while I soar. Love you for being you.

To everyone else who believed in the concept of this book and encouraged, supported, embodied the journey, and bravely said "Yes," in the absence of proof that we all will be changed for the better. I thank you.

Introduction

At first, this was going to be a different book.

I had decided to write about the loss of my granddaughter, Jaidin. I've learned so much and have written other books about the importance of not staying silent about trauma and heartache, so I wanted to tell Jaidin's story. Then I thought that women like me might also want to share with the world the gift of their beautiful grandchildren, as a way to honor those children and heal from such a heartbreaking loss. So I put out an invitation for others to join me, but no one else wanted to share that story.

Still, I felt sure that this book wasn't just for me and the story I wanted to tell, but I didn't know how that would work. So I waited and listened.

During this transition period, via conversation and social media, I noticed other silence-breaking stories, from other women I knew, bubbling to the surface. Some involved grief and loss, and some involved different suffering and challenges. All of these stories involved women overcoming.

I knew that Jaidin had come into my life to teach me something, although I certainly didn't know at the time what it would be. In the 16 years since her death, I've slowly learned the lessons she has for me, and this was another one: the chance to help others.

With Jaidin's help, I realized that maybe this book idea I'd had could be bigger than I first imagined, so I put the idea out there for other women to contact me if they wanted to share their own stories of overcoming, whatever that meant for them. This time, many women answered the call.

And viola! Sacred Hearts Rising was born.

To all the brave and beautiful women who stepped out of their comfort zones and broke the silence about the traumas of their pasts, I say: thank you. Know that you have decided to change the world in which we live in by sharing your stories.

What I find most inspiring about all of these stories is the healing journey that the writers have taken on. Some bravely came to Sacred Hearts Rising ready, for the first time, to write down stories and secrets they'd carried privately for decades. For others, this process was a journey back in time to revisit and clean out old wounds. And for some, this was the validation that they had completed their healing journey and that the old memories were now but thin ghosts of the past. None of these women are the same as when they started this process; they are forever changed.

Their hearts may have been broken, but they are rising. These women are moving forward into the lives that they deserve, and in these stories, they take you with them.

As in the beautiful image on the cover of this book, their pasts may have been torn and crumpled, and their feathers damaged and broken. But as they shed old memories and traumas, new experiences and insights come forth; damaged feathers fall, and new wings emerge.

I applaud every one of them for taking that first, second or hundredth step toward healing. Beyond their healing, every woman who shared her story did it for one main reason: to reach someone who may be going through what they'd gone through. They wanted to help others by sharing the light they'd found at the end of the tunnel, the hope they'd found for a better

Introduction

tomorrow and a brighter future, free from the pain of the past.

So to you the reader, I say: Welcome. You'll find so much grace in the pages of this powerful anthology. You'll read stories about various forms of abuse, grief, suicide, cancer, near-death experiences, mental illness and abandonment, and more. These are the stories that nobody wants to discuss. They are the hushed stories; the ones everyone wishes weren't there. But, they are. And they need to be told.

These stories need to be told because people need to know that they're not alone in their struggles that someone else understands what they're going through. Some of the stories may make you uncomfortable in your own skin; some will move you to tears and some maybe to enlightenment. As you read, you may find pieces of yourselves in these women, their strength and endurance to challenge what was expected of them and to break free into a whole new world, one that many didn't even know waited for them on the other side of the struggle.

None of us gets to walk through this life without having a challenge or two or three to overcome; how you decide to do that is solely up to you. You can cave into the abyss of the trauma, or you can decide that you deserve more than what you're getting. It's your choice.

Let the stories of all of these women speak to you wherever you are. If you're ready and willing, let them guide, inspire, and lead you to where you thought you might never go. Let them be your beacon of light on that often lonely road to healing. If you're a woman who isn't tormented by your past, then let this book teach you courage, forgiveness, and empathy, for we do not walk this earth alone.

So grab your favorite drink, have a seat, and visit these pages. I hope you are as amazed and inspired as I am at all of these women breaking the silence, and rising.

Foreword

By Jo Dibblee

Things happen. Remarkable, beautiful moments that fill my heart, and devastating, heartbreaking moments that bring me to my knees, challenge my resolve and make me ask why.

At times I yearn for the normal, in-between moments. Daily chores. Asking "what's for dinner?" When my adult children hug me for no apparent reason. Those normal moments, along with the occasional remarkably beautiful times, keep my reserves filled with grace and gratitude and help me navigate the heartbreak when it comes. Because it does come, as every woman in this book could tell you.

Have you ever found yourself so wholly devastated that you can't imagine standing back up? And still, somehow, from stuck knee-deep in the mud, you rose again to live?

I have, and although our circumstances are likely different, I'm guessing you have, too. How do we do this? I believe that it boils down to choice. Although we can't always control what happens, we can control how we react and respond.

Admittedly, it's hard to stand up after betrayal or devastation, no matter what the cause. A person's spirit can be so broken that she dare not take any action. At the same time, another person can stand with her brokenness and find the strength to serve others in the process.

I have nothing but compassion for those who are frozen in fear. For many years, that was me.

The line from the Robert Frost poem comes to mind: *"Two roads diverged in a wood, and I, I took the one less traveled by, and that has made all the difference."*

When I decided to stand for me and others, I was terrified to accept where I'd come from and to allow the truth of my life to come out. Letting go and letting be were among the hardest things I've ever done. At the same time, standing for myself and others likely saved my life. Doing so unleashed my purpose and fed my resolve to honor it.

Mine is the story of self-liberation from abject poverty, betrayal, assault, murder, and fear. All of which led to me to do my life's work. When I wrote Frock Off: Living Undisguised, I'd been in hiding for decades from an alleged serial killer and foster parent who used the system to access would-be victims, including myself.

I survived his assault and got away. Sadly, however, several years later, this man murdered Susan, a twelve-year-old girl I knew. When asked by the authorities if I would stand for Susan, I said yes. At age nineteen, I was willing to stand for her, but I wasn't yet willing or able to fully stand for myself.

This predator was never brought to justice, so for thirty-five years, I remained in hiding, fearful that he would do as he promised and finish the job with me. It wasn't an easy journey by any means, but knowing I was standing for Susan kept me going. She no longer had a voice, but I did!

Foreword by Jo Dibblee

For Susan and for me, in 2007, I decided to "Frock Off," that is to remove all manner of disguises and masks, to take back my life. It was a new beginning. A choice to get off of my knees, and out of the mud.

To stand back up, I needed a reason to rise. Susan and others whose voices had been silenced became my resolve, my why.

Each day I have a choice to start anew. Each day I decide how my life story will play out. Each day I am gifted with the same 86,400 seconds that are not to be squandered. Once gone, they are gone forever. You have these choices and gifts, too.

Of course, it's easier said than done to let go and let be, to heal from devastation and heartbreak. I've had to look deep in the belly of the beast for my own healing, but I've emerged stronger, more resilient, and wiser. I have a more profound sense of empathy and compassion.

In this anthology, you will read stories from other women who have healed and risen. You may be moved to tears and anger, and you'll see the common thread of resilience and optimism that runs through the stories of those who have not only endured, but also decided that life is a choice. When others might have chosen to stay put, these women have gotten back up. Like Brenda Hammon.

I met Brenda one day over pie. Well, I'd met her before that, in a larger group, but when we met over pie, it was different. I was able to see the calling Brenda had. I'm not sure if it was the pie because pie can be magical at times, but that day, I saw the essence of Brenda.

As I sat listening to Brenda share her story, I was struck by her bravery and uncanny ability to turn the darkest of the dark into something relatable and life-altering. Her heart was all in.

Soon Brenda was speaking at our live events, sharing her story and changing women's lives. I've learned that Brenda is a woman who knows what it takes to dig deep and find meaning in devastation. She is also a woman whose mission is to support others in doing so. She is real, raw and ready to be the change she wants to see in the world, and I'm proud to stand with her.

Sacred Hearts Rising is an anthology packed with the hope of those who have been brought to their knees, yet rose again. I love this book and all that it represents, and I'm so honored to offer these words to introduce it. For far too long, women have kept the stories of trauma and tragedy to themselves, our dirty little secrets. For far too long, we've been covered, concealed, and cloaked in fear and shame.

As a breakthrough expert, I work with women who often discover that when they stand and reclaim their lives, the secrets and fears of judgment no longer have the power. They do. You do. We do.

There's power in the stories we tell ourselves, and in unleashing the truth of our lives. There's power in the women who wrote the stories in this book, and power in you reading them. When we unite like this in cause and mission, we can ignite change.

Jo Dibblee
Frock-Off Inc. www.frockofflive.com
Four-time International Award Winning and Best-Selling author of "Frock Off: Living Undisguised."
Live Event producer of Best Kept Secret to Success in Life Love and Business

Sacred Hearts

She rises, rises from the cold
From the spirit of the fold
Passing, passing hearts on fire
Gifting wisdom through the wire

Pounding, pounding like a hoofbeat
Running, running blistered soul feet
Birthing life from old to newborn
Freeing souls between the death torn

She tears the ribbons from the telling
Sears the scars from monsters yelling
Calming screams with hands of softness
Lilting songs of hopeful deafness

Rising, rising like a storm
Mother Nature's child is scorned
Daughter, woman, youthful splendour
Gather round so we can mend her.

By Colleen Songs

Sacred Hearts Rising

Missing Footsteps

By Brenda Hammon

*A*round 10 pm on October 11th, I got the call that my daughter Tannis had delivered, by emergency C-section, a baby girl, and that the baby was in trouble. So much so that this little bundle was heading from Northern Alberta to the Children's Stollery Hospital in Edmonton, via an airplane. They'd named her Jaidin.

My heart dropped to the floor.

Tannis's husband Shilo shared that the baby was flying to Edmonton (where my husband and I lived), Shilo was driving the five and a half hours to get there, and that was because of the emergency C-section, Tannis had to wait for the next flight out. The first airplane couldn't wait while they stitched her back together. I couldn't fathom the pain that my daughter was going through. One minute you're having a baby and the next she's ripped from inside you and whisked away on an airplane. No warning, nothing.

My son-in-law asked, and I assured him that Bud and I would meet the ambulance at the hospital when little Jaidin arrived. My god, what a night-mare!

The minutes inched by in the Neonatal Unit in Edmonton as we waited

3

for Jaidin, and to find out any information as to what the problem was. I felt like a caged animal.

Finally, the nurses came out and told us that Jaidin had arrived and we could be with her. Bud and I rushed into the unit, and lying in the ICU bassinette was the most beautiful little girl I'd ever seen. I saw no signs that there was anything wrong with her—ten little toes and fingers, the face of an angel with two cute ears, a button nose, and perfect mouth. So what was wrong? Why was she here?

As I sat beside her, stroking her little hand, she wrapped her fingers around mine. My heart melted into a puddle of goo. I told myself over and over again that "she will be fine, that they will fix what I couldn't see and she will go home, happy and healthy."

Hours later when Shilo arrived, he looked like hell had won in a fighting contest with him. As he explained what the problem was with Jaidin, my heart broke into a million pieces and tears ran down my already wet cheeks.

Jaidin had been born with Autosomal Infantile Polycystic Kidney Disease, which meant that her kidneys were the size of a football, with cysts on every pore, which wasn't allowing waste to flow into her bladder. My little granddaughter couldn't pee, so therefore you couldn't feed her, which meant she was going to starve to death. The doctors had her on morphine already and were giving her small amounts of liquid, but not enough to make her have to drain her kidneys. They hoped that within a few days she would show signs of peeing; any amount would have been good.

We stayed with her most of the night, and when we finally went home to catch a few hours of sleep, I was exhausted. That following afternoon we met Tannis on the other side of the city at the Grey Nuns Hospital. She'd been flown to a different hospital because that's where they had an open bed, and her sister Martina had been able to fly with her. When we picked up the girls, Tannis was wearing only her hospital gown, so we stopped at the Southgate Mall on the way to the other hospital to get her a pair of pajamas. Since Tannis had had a C-Section, the Grey Nuns staff insisted that she return that evening.

I knew in my heart that wasn't going to happen. I knew that Tannis would remain by her daughter's side until Jaidin was able to go home, wherever Jaidin's home was going to be.

Within hours of her arriving in Edmonton, we had Tannis at the Children's Stollery Hospital, where she was able to see and hold Jaidin for the first time. Watching my daughter's eyes fill with hope for her baby was heartwarming and devastating at the same time.

I quietly left the room and headed for the chapel, where I sat and prayed to God to save Jaidin's life. I was never much about sitting and praying and wasn't even sure if I was doing it right, or if there was a right and wrong way. I had always talked to God but hadn't ever, I guessed, really prayed. That day, I prayed for a few hours, and the next day I slipped away and prayed some more, and the next day I prayed again, again, again.

All hope for Jaidin was slowly slipping away, so on the sixth day, I went back to that chapel, and I screamed at God to save her. I screamed until I couldn't scream anymore, I cried until all the tears were gone, and then I cried some more.

Finally, when I left the chapel, I knew that I'd done all I could, and I still had to be strong for my daughter who was going through the worst hell in her young life. I felt like such a failure. I couldn't even help my own child with her pain.

Jaidin was taken off life support and put in a private room. During the last hours of her life, we all took turns sitting with her, holding her and telling her that we loved her. As I held this amazing little person, I felt so blessed to be her grandmother, and that she had chosen us to be her family, to give her unconditional love and fight for her with every ounce of our beings.

Jaidin fought for hours to stay with her family but finally peacefully slipped away in the arms of her mother, the others who loved her standing vigil outside the room.

A week later, at Jaidin's funeral, I sat on the front bench looking at her beautiful picture, mounted in a frame beside all of her flowers. I still couldn't believe what had happened and that this little angel was gone forever, out of my life. The sadness consumed me.

Five years after Jaidin's passing, I was in a yoga class. At the time, my heart still ached with the pain of losing her, and it constantly ached for the pain that I couldn't help my daughter with. They say time heals all wounds, but it seemed like time hadn't healed mine so far, no matter how much yoga or anything else I did.

During the last phase of cool down and relaxation, I laid on the mat with my eyes closed, breathing in the cool air. For some reason, I turned my head to the left and opened my eyes, and there sat Jaidin smiling at me.

I didn't want to move or take my eyes off of her. I memorized her features as this five-year-old little girl, curly red hair cascading down her back, she sat with her arms wrapped around her knees, a little dress covering the tops of her knees. She smiled at me with a twinkle in her bright blue eyes. I can't explain it, but she told me she was okay and at peace.

My heart filled with so much love. It ached, but not in the same way. The pain I'd had was replaced with peace, knowing that Jaidin wasn't gone. That she still was around, watching us all from her place in heaven.

It's been over sixteen years since Jaidin came into my life, and not a day goes by that I don't think of her and wonder what she looks like, about her character, the sound of her laughter. I cherish every minute I have with her little sister, knowing that she's probably a lot like her big sister Jaidin, and I smile.

Brenda Hammon-Missing Footsteps

I wouldn't have wanted to miss the opportunity to have met Jaidin. Fleeting as our time together was, she has forever changed me. When I think of the strength of her spirit to try and conquer the obstacles placed in her path, and of the beauty and grace I saw in her as she did, I can't help but also think about how I want to face challenges in my own life. Jaidin fought for every day of life that she had, and I shall do the same.

I may not have been able to spend my whole life with Jaidin, but she got to spend her whole life with me and those who loved her. What more could a person ask for in life than to be loved unconditionally while they're here on earth?

I think about Jaidin often and how she's made me a better and wiser person. I've chosen that Jaidin will always be a part of my life.

I think about how old she is, and what she'd be doing if she was alive, and that in turn makes me cherish what I have.

I think about her first kiss, which makes me think about how I felt that first time, and I smile.

I think about her first horse—and with the horse-loving women she comes from, she definitely would've had one—and giving her words of encouragement. Again, I smile as I remember my first ride.

I think about her learning how to drive the quad. Then I remember teaching her little sister, and a few more gray hairs show up.

I think about her learning how to swim and dance as I watch our other grandchildren splash and twirl, and I smile.

I think about sleepovers, popcorn, and pizza, and again I smile as I watch the grandchildren enjoying their grandma time with me.

I think about her as I tell my crazy made up stories to the other grandchildren. I wonder if she's listening from the other side, and I smile.

I see Jaidin everywhere, in the beauty of living life. I've written her life and memory into this story, and she will never be forgotten. Since I am here and she is not, it is also my responsibility to live my life to the fullest and with purpose. While I'm here, I will not squander one moment, and when the day comes that I see her again, I will rejoice once more in seeing her beautiful face.

BIO: *Brenda Hammon*

Motivational speaker and philanthropist Brenda Hammon is the International Best Selling Author of Hear Me: No Longer Silent and I AM: Kicking Down the Walls of Silence, and an International Award Winner for I AM: Kicking Down the Walls of Silence. She believes that breaking the silence about sexual abuse and other topics usually cloaked in shame, is the only way to start the healing for victims and survivors.

Brenda is also the Producer and on-screen Executive Producer of the short film called, "A Shaft of Light: A Child Within." which was inspired by her books; "I Can't Hear the Birds Anymore," and "Hear Me: No Longer Silent." https://youtu.be/o2K8Rs1h6t8)

She is the Founder and CEO of Spirit Creek Publishing, Sacred Hearts Rising and www.brendahammon.com, where she inspires others to share their personal stories and helps other to publish their books. She posts to her site other author's books for no charge, and all books are linked to Amazon for purchase.

Brenda is always there to lend a helping hand to others when needed and has donated her books to worthy causes that empower and inspire women across Canada.

In the midst of her busy schedule, Brenda always takes time to ride her horse Hughie and to enjoy travel and gatherings with friends and family.

http://www.brendahammon.com
http://www.spiritcreekpublishing.com
http://www.spiritcreekfinancial.com
http://www.sacredheartsrising.com
https://www.facebook.com/brenda.hammon.9
Twitter: @HammonBrenda
LinkedIn: BrendaHammon

Roots

By Daphne McDonagh

When you see a beautiful tree out in nature, you may not see the twisted tangle of roots that lie beneath the surface.

This vibrant tree would not be what it is without these roots.

Although the roots may twist and turn, they have provided the tree with what it needs to grow. Such is life.

There may be many twists and turns along the way, but that is what we draw our best experiences from.

When life gets difficult, take a deep breath and know that everything will work itself out. It always does.

"A fatal car accident changed my life" is a loaded statement, packed with grief, agony, and healing. I never knew I could break a passenger window with my head and be pulled from the car before my mother even felt the impact. That is what happens when the car you are in gets broadsided.

Let me rewind for just a minute, and explain that two months before this event I was competing at a rodeo when I witnessed the love of my life, let's call him "D," die while bull riding. Even though I was only a teenager, I was sure that he was the one I was going to spend the rest of my life with. Little did I know that with him leaving so quickly it would be the best thing that could have happened!

On the way to the hospital from the accident scene, the ambulance attendance radioed into the hospital that I would be "Dead on Arrival" or DOA.

I am grateful that my dad said "No!" to the doctors when they wanted to immediately harvest my organs. My prognosis was guarded due to the significant neurological damage I sustained from the head injury. In a manner of moments, I had gone from being an athletic teen to being on full life support and in a coma.

As I lay in the hospital, between life and death, "D" came back to me. I cannot say that I saw or heard him; it was more like a knowing. The choice was mine to stay here on this earth or to be with my love again. He energetically helped me stay and remained with me as a protector for many years.

I can't tell you what discussion happened, but I have been told that the life support was discontinued after two weeks. To prevent further damage to my head; a tube was placed in a hole that was drilled through my skull. The tube was to drain the excess fluid off my brain and assist in relieving the pressure. I don't care what anyone says; sleep really is the best medicine. I know. I did it for eighteen days. In my heart, I know that even though the doctors did not see things improving, my loved ones knew that I would pull through.

Looking back now, I realize this car accident was bigger than me. There was definitely a higher power involved. Not only did this tragedy bring everyone in my life together, but it also helped me to see how strong I really was. Before the accident, I was a spitfire of a girl, who thought she had the world by the tail, only to realize that can be taken away in a flash.

I will never again take for granted being able to complete simple tasks like getting out of bed and walking down the hall while speaking to my family members.

Learning how to walk, talk, and feed myself again were the most difficult things I had ever done and it taught me what dedication and persistence are really about.

Giving up or quitting was never an option. Even though there were days that I had no idea how I was going to make it, I had chosen to be here, while I lay between life and death. So I thought I better buck up and get on with it.

Physically, I felt like I was a baby again. I knew what I wanted to do, but could not.

My left eyelid was only partially opened, and my eyeball was turned out to the side of my head. Part of my head was shaved from where the tube was, and I had scars all over my body from the glass. Emotionally, I went through many different stages during my recovery: fear, anger, hopelessness. I was sick and tired of all of the boring things I had to do over and over. So, I chose to do what I had to do to get out of the hospital. It was like a light bulb went off in my brain to commit to developing a game plan to do what I needed to do.

I will be forever grateful to the amazing rehabilitation team that poured in to help me even when I didn't want to work with them. I was in the hospital for only eight months, but my healing from this deep trauma continues to this day.

Just like the roots of a tree, I've had many twists and turns throughout the years since the accident, all of which brought me to now. I love looking back to see how the Universe provided me with what I needed exactly at the right me.

After going back to and graduating high school, I was living in a small town with a friend. Unhappy with the random work I was doing, I decided it was time for a change. I knew that there had to be more than shift work at a plant packaging scratch and win tickets, and I wanted to find it.

I was sure that working with people who had disabilities was my future. I was blessed to have come so far and becoming a member of society; I felt it was my turn to give back. The Rehabilitation Practitioner Program at Grant McEwan College came into my life via online searching. My roots twisted deeper.

Going back to school scared me and was not an easy choice after being in the work world, but I knew this was my next right move. I was able to access the services for students with disabilities which made the transition easier.

Funny enough, right around the same time I went back to college, I crossed paths again with a special guy I'd met a few years before. We dated for two years and then married after I graduated from the program. Our personalities truly still compliment and complete each other to this day.

I knew that I needed to focus on myself to get better before I could help anyone else. I was braving the pain while I worked with others with disabilities. I find it simply amazing how the Universe brings us the perfect people and the right moment.

I wasn't looking for anyone who could help me when I was introduced to this wonderful acupuncturist who became the conduit for the second part of my healing journey. At the time, I was petrified of needles but wanted to give it a shot, because I was always dealing with so much pain. Interestingly enough, her needles caused my headaches to slow down and my pain levels to decrease after only two or three treatments.

I was still working in the field of rehabilitation when I stumbled on to the Animal Science Diploma. It was a course I could do online while still working. I loved how it challenged me on a whole new level.

A bit of back-story here: ever since I could talk I said I was going to be a large animal veterinarian, but after coming back from the car accident and a massive closed head brain injury, I needed to rethink my options. I learned many new skills in this program but realized that it wasn't the direction I needed to go.

Seeing and being around all of the sick animals brought my energy and spirit down. The animals were sharing with me what was wrong. I would hear and feel their pain in my body, but I was limited to what I could do to assist. When I told the people that I could help them with their animals, they shrugged me off like I had no idea what I was talking about.

The one thing I loved about the rehab field was the diversity. I liked looking outside the box at new ways of getting things done. I loved the many different jobs I did and people I met, but this is also what pushed me away from the field. I began to see that although there were many that wanted help in learning to do things independently, there were also many who didn't want my help. I never stopped looking for new ways to help others.

I was already aware that magnets helped me live with less pain, but I didn't know why. That was when The Healing with Crystal Therapy Course presented itself. It was wonderful as I was not only finding more and more ways to help myself feel better, but also seeing the infinite possibilities to help others too. As I worked my way through this course, I saw that I knew a lot about what they were teaching. It felt like I was being reminded instead of learning something new. I began to tap into my innate ability to channel energies both negative and positive while working with both animals and people.

I was still getting a strong pull to move away from the rehab field, but I had no idea what I wanted to do. I kept growing my roots deeper.

I had my Rehabilitation Practitioner, Animal Science, and Healing with

Crystal Therapy Diplomas. Three completely unconventional modalities, but they all fit together so well. I learned many valuable skills from these different courses, and I was ready to put them to great use. So, I chose to go the world of banking.

Yes, I realize that those diplomas seem to have no connection to banking, but it was fascinating how I brought everything together!

I was so out of my comfort zone when I started at the bank, but deep down I knew there was a reason I was there. It was very challenging for me, but once I found my groove, I soared. The step by step routines I was taught way back when I was in the hospital came in very handy at the bank. The interpersonal skills I learned in the rehab field assisted me to communicate with clients at the counter. My manager was wonderful. He helped me to gain skills to stand tall and speak my mind. He never gave up on me and reminded me to see just because tasks were always done one way that didn't mean I had to do it that way, too. He empowered me to see there was always another way; all I had to do was look for it. My roots twisted with this new path but still grew deeper.

While working in the bank, I was a secret crystal carrier. Not many knew of my past, and I was not yet ready to tell them about everything I had been through and all of my abilities. I was worried they might have me committed. My commute to work was long, which gave me time to connect with my guides. Since before the accident, I have always been able to connect with my guides, I never really gave it much thought. To be completely honest, I have no way to explain how or why I can. I Just Do It.

I was still working in the bank but was now sharing my secrets with more people, and much to my surprise many were open to seeing more information about what the crystals and energy moving could do. The Universe was ready to provide me with the next steps in my journey when I was ready to step into my true being.

So that I didn't need to carry bags of rocks in my pockets, I began making jewelry with the crystals. Once I had an outrageous number of magnetic, crystal earrings, my husband suggested I show them to my friends. He thought they might like them.

I was beginning to see the endless possibilities again. I love how the Universe provides the next step when a person is ready. Who knew that a hobby of making crystal healing jewelry, when I chose to stop smoking, would turn into my full-time job of owning and operating Daphne's Healing Hands!

When I asked the Universe, "How does it get any better?" divine synchronicities lined up more opportunities. For instance, a customer walked into the bank carrying something that had this magical light shining from it. What I noticed led to a conversation with this customer about crystal therapy, and I learned how to incorporate this, along with light therapy, into my healing practices. This began the next step in my journey, and the roots grew deeper still. I was handed the opportunity to be able to assist with not only crystal therapy I was now able to help people with the light therapy as well.

Looking back, when I was that teenage girl in the hospital bed, I could not have predicted how blessed I was and would be. Choosing to come back from a massive closed head brain injury was the toughest and most rewarding decision I have ever made.

Now, I am honored to help both people and animals release and let go of what they no longer need to carry. I am grateful to wake with excitement daily for the next opportunity the Universe is going to present. Like a sturdy tree, I have learned to bend and sway with the wind of storms. My beautiful roots grow stronger and deeper every day.

BIO: *Daphne McDonagh*

For many years, Daphne has helped both animals and people to let go of unnecessary energetic baggage they are carrying. She helps them life on purpose and without pain, both physical and emotional. Daphne especially loves assisting pets and their owners' transition through the releasing process together.

Drawing from her diverse educational background, including Rehabilitation, Animal Science, and Crystal and Cold Laser Therapies she balances, restores, and rejuvenates energies.

This is her first published piece of writing. You can learn more about her services at www.daphneshealinghands.com

Website: www.daphneshealinghands.com
https://www.facebook.com/DHHCrystalCreations/
Twitter: d_healing
C: 780-238-7208 (call or text)
E: daphne@daphneshealinghands.com

The Decision That Changed My Life

By Becky Norwood

Since first deciding to share my story, only one year ago, my life has transformed in dramatic ways. I am by far happier, at peace with life and I have been able to help others achieve the same. But before I go there, let me share with you the events that transpired in my life long before I even dreamed that change was possible.

My abuse probably started when I was a baby at the hands of my father. My mother was an abused mess, who had married at barely seventeen and had never learned to stand for herself, let alone her children. Her coping mechanism was being sick all the time.

It is a true blessing for many abuse victims/survivors that our memory or lack thereof serves us well! My earliest recollections begin the night I decided to run away from home at four years old, on the streets of Los Angeles, CA. That evening, before my father arrived from work, I was setting the dinner table. As I did, I kept circling the table chanting, "I will not cry, I will not cry." Endlessly, I cried when my father came in from work. It always ended in a spanking that resembled a beating.

This night, I decided I had had enough. My evening chores completed, I slipped out the back door unnoticed and ran as fast as my legs would take me. I got about ten blocks from home when I stopped. I suddenly realized that I had no idea where I was, or where I would go. As I began to cry, an elderly couple out for their evening stroll stopped to inquire where my parents were. In retrospect, if my five-year-old grandson were all alone ten blocks away, I'd not be a happy camper. This couple took me home.

My father graciously thanked them, but what they saw and what I received after that was in stark contrast. He beat me the entire rest of the night, insisting I would not be crying again, nor would I ever run away again. Every time I stopped crying, he beat me again. From that night on, my fire may not have burned out completely, but I remember deciding that I would always obey him, no matter what he asked of me.

To this day, I do not recall what events led me to the decision to run away, or why I cried every time he came near me, but I do remember many events after that fateful night. Suffice it to say; I was not the only one that experienced the wrath of my father.

For my siblings and me, beatings were a regular occurrence. Isolation was constant. Sexual abuse was common. Verbal abuse the likes of which I witnessed grown men crumble under, let alone his children and his wife. The insidious mental abuse was what kept us always at his beck and call. Religion played a huge role, as no matter which religion he chose to follow, (he chose a variety of different religions as I was growing up), his charismatic nature always sent him to the top to carry out roles of authority. To see him stand before a congregation and preach on proper behavior, was not only painful but incredibly confusing.

The only individual I could equate him to is Hitler. Playing was not for his children; we were there to serve. I was serving as mother to my siblings by the age of eight. At one point, I witnessed him take a broom handle, and break every one of my sister's toes. Why? She failed to accomplish a chore in the manner he prescribed.

20

With this kind of framework, I entered adulthood with a mixture of baggage. My heart wanted what was good and right for me, but I felt that I did not deserve it. I was not "clean and pure," therefore what good man would want me?

As with most survivors, I attracted what I knew. For a period of my life, I was promiscuous, as sex meant the person most certainly loved me, and I was searching for love. In all the wrong places, in all the wrong ways. With the sexual abuse of my childhood, it was the only time my father was gentle and kind to me, and I came to prefer the sexual abuse over the beatings, verbal and mental abuse.

Eventually, I attracted the same abusiveness I had known from my father, in the man I chose to marry. He became the father of my children. My marriage to him lasted only three years, but the gift I received from that marriage was two amazing daughters whom he chose not to support or love.

Now, a single mom, I worked hard to provide a solid framework for my daughters. I loved being a mom. I stayed single for twenty years, simply because I was afraid of attracting the same thing into my life. I worked hard on myself, and as I raised my little family, I came to find the strength that I had not known was in me. The goodness and the fire in me had not completely extinguished! While I know, I made my share of mistakes as I figured myself out, slowly I became more comfortable in my own skin.

My relationship with my father was tenuous at best. To protect my family, I distanced us from him as best I could. One Sunday afternoon, he knocked at my door asking to speak to me.

By this time, he had become a very angry, sad and depressed man with no drive for anything, except heavy drinking to numb the pain. During the conversation we had, he said to me, "Becky, you have broken the pattern in our family." To which I replied, "What pattern is that?" His response was, "The pattern of abuse in our family, and I am very proud of you. You do

21

not beat your children, you are such an excellent mother, and you parent them in a way that you shows them love and respect."

Shocked at his comment, I responded, "Abuse does not work, Dad. It doesn't make anyone a better person." As I thanked him for acknowledging me, I knew this was the greatest gift he had ever given to me.

Some two months later, when my children were just nine and ten, he took his life. His suicide had a huge impact on my little family, in so many ways. As my mom and siblings came to together after his death, we began to talk. Ironically, while we all knew of the mental, emotional, physical, verbal, and even spiritual abuse we had suffered at our father's hand, not one of us knew the other had experienced abuse sexually. Shockingly, even my brother had experienced sexual abuse! Silence and fear had kept us from disclosing this deep dark secret. We had each thought that we were the only ones who had suffered from sexual abuse. As we talked, I was the first one to broach the subject.

We each had been threatened with not only our own lives but the lives of our entire family if we dared to speak. We ALL believed him and knew him to be capable of carrying out his threats. As I shared my story with my siblings, the tears began to flow. One by one, my siblings confessed to experiencing the same, and the impact it had on our lives.

In the next three years, our family experienced two more suicides. Twenty years later, the aftermath still carries its toll, with two more family members choosing the same way out. Abuse had a long history, one that went back generations in our family. The aftermath is not pretty.

For me, while on the one side of the coin, it was a relief to no longer be harassed by the man that was our father, the flip side of all this is that the pain of the shadows of my past would revisit often. It was tough to know how to answer my daughter's questions and needs, and still deal with my own emotions. The first few years after his suicide was terribly difficult for all of us. I could maintain well for long periods of time; then something would trigger the feeling the shame, grief, depression and the memories of fear that I had suffered.

While I did a great job raising my daughters, (they are incredible women now in their thirties), I regret that they had to experience not only suicide but knowing the kind of man their grandfather was. They were so young when this happened, and no child should have to face such issues. EVER! While healing has come to our family, I know that there are still residuals of pain for all of us. It has been a long journey.

My mother has since remarried, and healing has taken place for her as well. She is certainly healthier now in her 80's than I ever knew her to be in her youth. Being sick was her way to cope when I was a child. She and I have worked hard to mend our hurt hearts and let the past be the past as best we can.

The demons would come to haunt me like a heavy wet blanket descending over my head. Shame kept me quiet. I could not let the outside world know that underneath the smile and apparent success, the smile I bravely wore could easily be turned upside down with the words, "You are ugly, stupid, and will never amount to anything," that I heard practically every day of my young life.

Nearing my sixties, I decided that the waves of depression that would wash over me had to stop. Look what I had going for me! After twenty years as a single mom, I married an amazing man who simply loved me for me. Not long after we met, I told him of my past. I knew he should know what he was dealing with, figuring he would take the nearest exit. Happily, he did not.

Instead, he quietly stood by my side, offering strength and kindness I had never known. His love and support have been constant, and we celebrate ten years of marriage and many blessings. We blended our two families with five adult children and now enjoy twelve grandchildren and a life that is very blessed.

When we first married, my husband would often shake me awake at night saying that I was sobbing in my sleep. I had no idea. Now he tells me that only on rare occasions does it startle him awake, and then only for a brief moment.

He and I often spoke of writing my story as a way of processing my past. I always thought it to be a good idea, but sitting down and writing those words was quite another thing. Finally, a very dear friend and I had a very pointed discussion on the subject. She asked me, "How long are you going to keep this bottled up inside of you? It's time!"

I finally committed to writing my story. As I wrote, I began to unravel the stories, events, memories and the pain. As the days passed and my story unfolded, my heart became lighter. It was the breath of fresh air I had never experienced before this. It was as if, in the writing of my story, I began to write a new story for my life.

For me, it was like magic, and in that magic, my life is different now from what I ever dreamed possible. I am happy, grounded and successful. I will not say that life does not bring triggers that set me back from time to time. That would not be the truth and quite unrealistic. Life has a way of doing that.

Life is truly good for me now. I have found a new frame of reference and a much better way to handle those times. I also feel that it came down to a decision I had to make. I had to decide that I would take the steps necessary to change the way I react and respond to life. I had to decide to live the life I am living now.

With some trepidation, I decided to publish my story in August of 2016, in celebration of my 60th birthday. In my wildest of dreams, I would not have ever expected the response I received. It came from people I knew and from complete strangers. Many thanked me for having the courage to tell my story and for the perspective in which I wrote it. Touched and in awe of the responses I received, it became a further source of healing.

Knowing it made a difference for men and women alike, gave me strength and confidence.

Discovering I was not alone in what I experienced was likewise a source of healing. Due to isolation and shame, I had not understood that childhood sexual abuse was such a staggering epidemic in our world. Most of us do not know that. Not only have many gone to their grave bearing the weight of the shame, guilt, and fear that causes the silence, many still living are quietly burdened with the pain.

Now, as I speak to audiences, I can see it in the faces of the women listening to me. Publishing my story in my book; "The Woman I Love–Surviving, Healing, and Thriving After a Childhood of Sexual, Emotional and Physical Abuse," has helped many women discover their voices, and begin to stand up for themselves, finding their inner truth, strength, and joy.

Who would have known that the deepest pain of my past could have turned into the rich, rewarding, fulfilling life I now enjoy? My message to anyone who can relate to and fit into the shoes I once wore: If you are currently in an abusive situation, get help immediately. If the abuse is now behind you physically, but still walks with you in your daily life, coloring your world less than joyful, seek help! Life is simply too short, and there is so much joy, beauty, and satisfaction that comes from deciding to heal and to thrive.

Each of us that do make that decision make a difference for others who will follow us. If we can hold the light high for them, extend our hand and lift them up on a journey of healing, it will become a ripple effect, felt all the way into the families, communities, and the world where we live.

BIO: *Becky Norwood*

Becky Norwood is an International Best-Selling Author, Speaker, Coach, and Book Publishing Expert. She is also the architect of Your New Story Blueprint. She has worked with over thirty clients to become best-selling authors, helping them to establish their credibility and expertise and leave a lasting legacy.

Women, who have been living a "rearview mirror" life, playing that same story over and over again, hire Becky to discover their true inner strength, values, and life's purpose. She helps them find the key to unlocking the power of rewriting their story so that they can dramatically change the perspective of their past.

The Woman I Love on Amazon: http://amzn.to/2F8c1NM
We Choose to Thrive: Our Voices Rising in Unison to Share with Abuse Survivors a Message of Hope and Inspiration: http://amzn.to/2CXYMON
www.thewomanilove.com
https://www.facebook.com/thewomanilove1/ (Facebook page)
https://www.facebook.com/groups/thewomanilove/ (private group)

Today I Am Free

By Patsy Davis

*A*fter fifty odd years of searching for love, I've found it in myself. I'm living alone and learning to trust someone: me. This aloneness doesn't mean giving up on relationships. It's about me. Now, I also have love to give. It may be too late for some of my relationships, but for others, I know it's just the right time.

To reach this point of loving and trusting myself, I had to reconnect with a traumatic childhood incident.

I was two and a half years old, the second youngest in a family of eight children. We were at the lake for a typical Sunday picnic after church. I think my Dad decided to make a game of getting everyone into the car that day, and you can imagine the effort that took with seven of us children and two adults.

My next memory is of me, in my brown dress, chasing the car, running as hard as I could, legs and arms pumping as I tried to catch it, choking on dust, tears, and screams. Why can't they see me? Why don't they hear me?

The car is out of sight. I keep running as fast and as far as I can.

Although I was little, I thought I was mighty! I ran and ran. In my mind, I planned to cut across the woods and beat them home. When I reached the concession stand at the entrance to the park and headed across the road to cut through the woods, people who recognized me stopped me. "No! No! Let me go," I yelled. "I have to get home." Although their only intent was to get me safely back to my family; I didn't understand that. I fought them with every ounce of energy I had left.

A sibling later told me that when Dad realized I wasn't in the car, although they were on a narrow, gravel road, he never even slowed down but "burned a turn" and headed back to the lake to find me.

This whole incident happened so quickly, likely within the space of an hour, but it's stayed with me my whole life.

I don't recall being reunited with my family, or how they felt. I do know that the trauma of the event has overshadowed most of my life, leaving me terrified of being abandoned. A few years after the incident, I almost drowned, and those were my two strongest childhood memories. Otherwise, I only remember feeling that I didn't belong.

As a teenager, trying to "fit in," I tried it all: smoking, drugs, alcohol, running away from home, being sexually active, trying so hard to feel wanted, acknowledged and accepted. I ached to feel like I belonged somewhere. At sixteen, I left home and was on my own, working and partying.

Married at seventeen to someone I'd known for a while, I had my daughter at eighteen. Shortly after her birth, I started having nightmares. I'd wake up paralyzed with fear, unable to move or to speak. I vividly remember one time trying to scream and roll over to wake my husband but was unable to do so.

What was going on?

To compound the situation, my marriage wasn't one in which I felt safe to share emotionally, but I'm not sure I even knew how to do that. This was the first time I sought out a counselor. I drove seventy miles to secret appointments, but that was short-lived due to the shame I felt at having to seek help.

Ten years later, when my husband wanted to make a move that felt too risky and isolating for our two young children and me, I decided to leave my marriage. Having moved the kids and me to our own place, I was terrified and felt lost. Soon, my husband and I reunited, although nothing in the relationship had changed.

A few years later, after a move to a different province and a new home, I was still miserable in the marriage and again sought out counseling. I knew something was missing; I wanted a better way to live. At the time, I was watching John Bradshaw's PBS programming on healing shame while connecting with your inner child, and I heard about a weekend retreat, based on his work, being offered in our area. I felt I needed to go.

During one of the group exercises on reclaiming our inner child, a vivid picture of my young self, this little girl in a brown dress, and all the terror she felt at the lake came rushing back to me. At some level, I've always known that moment had been life-changing.

At the retreat and afterward, I still wasn't ready to process such powerful emotions. I shut down the feelings of fear and abandonment, so I didn't have to acknowledge and deal with my pain. This also translated to not acknowledging my worth. I stayed stuck in fight or flight mode, always needing to defend myself or be in control. I could meet the physical needs of my children, but when it came to a deep emotional connection with them, I just couldn't let go or relax enough to allow that to happen.

Several years after the retreat, I talked to my Mom about being left behind at the lake. I was unable to do much but cry as the emotions spilled out into a difficult conversation for us both. Mom told me that I was inconsolable that day and for months afterward, but they didn't know what to do for me. On some level, this was validating evidence that something traumatic had happened to me. Still, I didn't know what to do with it.

When I was thirty-something, the feeling of not belonging intensified. I felt invisible and silent. I couldn't even see or hear myself. I wanted to disappear. Several times I contemplated suicide, but somehow knew that wasn't the answer. Once, when we were living in the Okanagan, and some of my husband's family was visiting, we drove down across the border to shop. The urge to disappear was so strong that I left the store and walked away. I went several blocks before stopping, realizing I couldn't do this to my children.

Shortly after this, my husband told me he was having an affair. This was an extremely painful time in my life. We limped along in the marriage for another year or so, and I finally decided that it was time to move on.

Soon, I was separated with two teenagers, and no idea of how to make a life. I still hadn't dealt with my childhood pain and found myself caught up in another relationship. This caused a rift between my teenagers and me, and they chose to go live with their dad. Again, I felt abandoned. For a time, the kids wouldn't even speak to me. We were living in a small town, and one day walking down Main Street, I saw my daughter and a couple of friends walking towards me. I was thrilled, only to be devastated as they crossed the street, it seemed, to avoid me. Maybe I was invisible.

I threw myself into the new relationship. Up until that point, it had been long-distance, with lots of phone calls and letter writing, so I decided to move and see if we had a chance. It didn't take long for us to join our lives together.

This was the second marriage for both of us, and we entered it with trepidation and love, planning on overcoming the odds.

For several years, life was full. Still searching for more, I was in and out of counseling. This time, my new husband encouraged me to go, and I didn't feel the need to keep it a secret. About four years ago, during a session, the abandonment I felt as a result of that childhood incident resurfaced, and finally, I could process the emotions. 'Feeling' into the fear and grief changed who I am and how I look at life.

Regrettably, it also put a huge stress on my marriage, and just recently my spouse and I separated. While I'm still hopeful that we can come back around to each other, I'm grateful for the gifts of my current circumstances.

Living alone without the fear of not fitting in, or being abandoned and living alone with the feeling that I can support myself, has been one of the most empowering times of my life. It's not about being free of a relationship, but rather feeling free to figure out who I am. For the first time, I feel confident and content with me.

All my life I felt like a round peg in a square hole, afraid to speak up yet, desperately wanting to be seen and heard. I remember now that as a child I'd wanted to be famous, likely because then I'd never be forgotten or left behind. As an adult who felt unworthy, I denied myself in many ways— from not buying clothes, not getting the expensive dental work I needed in my twenties, to not allowing myself to experience joy or pleasure as I didn't believe I was worth it.

Counseling brought me a long way, but the real healing began as I started to tell other women what had happened to me as a child, and they acknowledged my pain.

Wow.

Since this incident hasn't ever been discussed within my family, my feelings about it were surrounded by shame. Now I could finally let that go. As the healing continues, I'm finally recovering happy memories and find myself reclaiming my childhood.

Am I the only one who has felt unworthy and alone, so unloved and invisible? Probably not.

As I travel this road to healing, I'm learning that many of us have experienced events in our lives that may seem insignificant, but which have formed who we are.

I spent a lifetime making decisions based on a lie, based on a story I made up about what happened to me all those years ago, one I lived unconsciously: "I'm not worthy. I'm not loveable. No one wants me; everyone leaves me. No one cares what happens to me."

Learning the truth—that I am worthy, loveable, and wanted, that even if I'm abandoned again, I can look after myself—has been amazing. Today, able to process emotions I've suppressed for years, I'm able to express myself in loving ways, adopting and understanding self-care and compassion towards myself and to others, including my children.

I will soon be sixty years young and never expected to feel the freedom I do today. That little girl is all grown up now, and ready to live life to the fullest. No more living on the sidelines, no more fearing the worst but now expecting the best. As I rebuild and deepen the relationships with my children and my family, I am learning to say "YES" to living life and to experiencing its challenges, knowing most of all, that I am worthy of love.

BIO: *Patsy Davis*

Patsy Davis is the second youngest of eight children, and now mother to two accomplished adult children, and grandmother to two beautiful granddaughters. Today, Patsy is an entrepreneur, building a successful Bookkeeping Business and learning to say yes to life.

As a Certified Professional Bookkeeper, she enjoys supporting and empowering business owners by ensuring they have the financial information they need to make informed business decisions.

Learning to laugh and love life after years of feeling lost and left behind, Patsy actively seeks opportunities to connect and share her story with women who may have experienced personal trauma, due to what others perceive as "insignificant" events in their lives. Inspired by her own healing and newfound feeling of freedom, Patsy yearns for all women to live lives free of fear and shame.

Sacred Hearts Rising

I Heard Your Voice

By Marta Clay

*M*y nine-year-old was having a meltdown, again, and I was close to having one myself, which isn't extremely beneficial to a positive outcome. Soon after, through the guidance of an acquaintance, we learned that Kurtis has Asperger's Syndrome and Sensory Processing issues. Meltdowns, over-reactiveness to the teasing from others, etc. was a normal day for us.

We began our education in this new-found frontier and decided the first step was to enlist the aid of a psychologist to help us deal, in an appropriate manner. We found the ideal person that fit Kurtis' needs, and he began to see her once a week. After each of his sessions, I would be allowed to come in, hear what progress had been made, and what we could do as "homework" until meeting again. Things like purposefully attempting eye contact, or waiting for a person to respond to a topic being discussed, were the things Kurtis needed to hone his skills on.

January 17, 2008, is an afternoon that will be forever etched in my mind. It was a Thursday because that was the day of each week that school ended early, and I planned Kurtis' appointments with his psychologist, Kara, on those days.

On this particular day, a raw wind blew with such intensity that my cheeks felt like they were on fire, even though the sun was shining. The session began as usual, with Kara coming out to the waiting area to escort Kurtis to her office, and to spend a few moments with me, to see if there were any issues that needed to be known before his time began.

All went like clockwork, until halfway through the allotted time; Kara came to me, visibly shaken. She informed me that there was a situation that needed to be handled immediately.

At first, I couldn't quite understand what was happening, because this was so out-of-the-ordinary. For some strange reason, I automatically thought that someone had been, or was, molesting my child, and I wondered, "Who am I going to have to kill?" Then the self-talk began. I made a quick decision that I should not break down or show emotion in front of Kurtis. He wouldn't need that on top of everything else he was going through.

I made it to Kara's office, and found my son, clearly upset, with a tear-stained face, and not looking at me when I entered the room. To me, it was clearly a sign that someone had touched him in an unsavory way. I don't remember breathing, at this point, because the room was so deadly quiet, and a feeling of sadness was there.

Kara broke the silence by asking Kurtis if he wanted to tell me why I had been asked to participate in the session, earlier than usual.

He quickly denied her request, and she proceeded to tell me what I never dreamed I would hear.

At the tender age of nine, my baby wanted to kill himself. He could not tolerate, any longer, the way kids were treating him at school, and had had enough. He so wanted to be friends with them, but they weren't treating him like a friend, at all, and he couldn't understand what was happening.

My heart broke with the knowledge of this development, but I maintained my composure.

When everything had been revealed, Kara asked Kurtis, "Why didn't you want to tell your mom?"

He said, "I was afraid she would be mad at me."

My first response was an inner shame that my child was frightened of the retribution he might receive from me. Then I lost control, and I cried. Not the convulsing sobs I so desperately wanted to have, but tears streamed steadily down my face, and I quickly allayed any thoughts, from his mind, that I would be angry with him for being so desperately upset. I told Kurtis, "Oh, honey, Mama could never be mad at you for that." I felt like I had been running for my life and could barely breathe.

The immediate discussion and recommendation by Kara was to make everyone with daily contact with him, aware of the situation he found himself in. First and foremost was Kurtis' school, for two reasons: the faculty was with him for more of his waking hours than I was, and because of the way he'd imagined ending his life was to jump from the top of a school building. This was pivotal because of where it was to happen, and since Kurtis was afraid of heights that he would even consider such a thing.

The session went much longer than usual, and Kara canceled the rest of her appointments so that we had adequate time for discussions and strategies. My knees were trembling uncontrollably, and my feet had no desire to move forward. And, if the truth is known, I don't think I could have walked from that room under my own power at that moment.

To be honest, I thought I was prepared when I left her office that dark, cold afternoon. But the twenty-minute drive home seemed forever. I could hardly wait to get to my sanctuary, not realizing it would feel like a prison once I got there.

See, I didn't count on not knowing how to "do life" with a child who would rather be dead than live the life he was living. After returning home, I started dinner, but couldn't keep my mind on violently chopping the vegetables for a salad and scrubbing the thin, brown skin of the potatoes. I was too busy making sure Kurtis was okay and not hurting himself until my husband could arrive home and we could become a tag-team.

With dinner prepared, eaten, and dishes done, my husband and I attempted to make the evening as normal as any other. For me, normal it was not because I was constantly checking to see what Kurtis was doing. Finally, it was bedtime, which was a blessing for a short time, but then, became a nightmare. Throughout the night, grabbing a blanket to shield myself, I would cautiously descend the dark stairway to Kurtis' bedroom. I would linger at the doorway of his room, looking beyond the stack of books and dinosaur figures, relieved to find him in bed, with his little chest, rising and falling, and hearing a faint snore that signified all was well in dreamland.

Each day became a little easier to cope with this realization, and for me to get over the fact that this was not about me. The initial days into this, I was selfish and wanted people to feel sorry for me. Why was no one coming to my side, and asking how they could help me through this?

After wallowing in this pity pool of mine, I came to terms that I wasn't the only person who had ever experienced this. And I came to realize, when Kurtis returned to the very busy child I loved, that I was most fortunate because he was still alive, and working to resolve his issues.

To say that everything has been sunshine and flowers since would be a blatant lie. For a time, the teachers and administration at the private school that Kurtis attended seemed to be as concerned about him as we were. But, I found rather quickly, that they didn't have his best interest at heart. After an incident at school, Kara strongly recommended that we pull him from their institution, and thus began my teaching career, which lasted until he graduated at the age of sixteen.

With the new-found freedom of homeschooling, we were able to delve into acquiring the knowledge of things that could be done to make life smoother for Kurtis and our family life in general. As before, he continued to see Kara but also started seeing Kathy, an Occupational Therapist, to help with sensory processing issues.

We've tried everything that was suggested or even hinted at, to help make a difference in Kurtis' life. Besides seeing Kara and Kathy, throughout the years, Kurtis has also participated in Social Skill classes, Animal-Assisted therapy, Hippotherapy (horses), Acupuncture, and Listening therapy. With all these things occurring, our life has been extremely busy, but so worth the effort and end-results.

Kurtis has found his passion in life as a Voice-Over Artist after dallying with the ideas of owning a restaurant that catered to children's likes and developing video games. Now he's twenty-years-old, has a recording studio, a thriving business, and four years under his belt in this business. Kurtis knows I have his back, and there is nothing that we can't talk about. There are no taboo subjects.

Over the years, my role as a mom has evolved, too. At times, it seems this striking episode in Kurtis' childhood never occurred. But, there are times when some small event, will cause all the old feelings and fears to come flooding back. Kurtis is a loner, and with that, I become afraid that he will do something to harm himself. He has learned that his mama needs to see his joking side, several times a day to qualm those fears. Plus, I've had to learn that this is Kurtis' personality and doesn't mean he is upset or brooding.

Has being Kurtis' mom been easy? No! Would I change anything that I've experienced? Most likely not. If we hadn't gone through this together, our bond wouldn't be as strong as it is, and we wouldn't be the people we are today. Shifting from fearing for his life to applauding his development into the young man he is today, makes all the heartache and worry so worth it.

As a mom, I still worry, as all moms do. While this chapter of life has come to an end, the rest of the book remains to be written. Will it all be smooth sailing? Of course not! I know one day I may find myself in another room being told something scary and hard to comprehend that will require all my love, creativity, and smarts to survive, but I also know what I'm made of, and that I will be ready.

BIO: *Marta Clay*

With nineteen years of experience in the financial services industry, Marta Clay is a Senior Vice President Partner with Primerica Financial Services. Members of the Financial Independence Council with Primerica, she and her husband, recently received the company's highest award; they were inducted into the Wall of Fame.

Originally from Little Rock, Arkansas, Marta currently resides in Edmonton, Alberta, with her husband, Don, and son, Kurtis. They enjoy traveling extensively and spending quality time with family, and the friends they've acquired since moving to the Great White North.

Marta's passion is to help people's dreams come true. She accomplishes this through her family's financial service endeavor. Also, as a natural planner, she's spent many years designing once-in-a-lifetime events for momentous occasions in her friends' and family's lives.

Sacred Hearts Rising

I'm Not Crazy

By Martina Soderquist

My heart starts to race, thumping in my chest, I feel my skin crawling preventing me from sitting still, I can't take a deep breath. I twist and scratch my fingers, rocking back and forth on the couch. I'm sweating, and my chest feels like it's in a vice, slowly robbing me of my breath. The little voice in my head says, "You are weak, you are alone, this is bigger than you, you won't survive. Why aren't you normal? Why do you have to be like this?"

Every muscle in my body aches from tension. I start to cough, then make a mad dash to the bathroom, barely reaching the toilet before the vomit comes. Tears stream down my face, no longer able to be contained. I think to myself, "I can't stay here, or I will die." The feeling is so raw, so real. I am trapped. Helpless. A prisoner of my mind.

Somehow I manage to call my sister, who just dropped me off at my home. She tells me to come to her house.

The only thought in my mind is, "get to her house; then you will be okay."

I'm shaking, and my breath comes in short spurts as I back out of my parking spot, not caring that I hit the "Do Not Park" sign.

The next thing I recall is stilling on my sister's couch wrapped in a blanket. She's scared. She's never seen me this bad, so she texts mom and they both decide that I need to go to the emergency room.

I will always remember that day. It was my second day in a full-blown panic. No relief. My sister described my anxiety as watching the mercury rise in a thermometer, the closer we got to my house the more my attack intensified. I was scared of being alone and what would happen to me if nobody was around.

What led to this low point was the ending of a psychologically, verbally and emotionally abusive relationship. It was one of the darkest periods in my life. The anxiety, depression, and panic attacks crippled me. I existed only, living in a shroud of darkness, fear, and wanting to die.

Most people can relate to feeling anxious, but I'm not talking about being anxious. I'm talking about a debilitating anxiety disorder that makes the basic life skills difficult to manage. Worrying over day to day activities, fearing the anxiety, fearing the depression, and fearing the panic attacks. Being in such pain and unable to see a way out except to die. Terrified of being alone. What happens if I panic again?!

When my mom and sister decided I needed to go the hospital, the Physiatrist on call in the ER put me on Zoplicone a sleeping pill and Clonazepam a sedative. He also increased the Pristiq I was taking to a higher dosage. I chose not to stay in the hospital that night. I was terrified of being alone, even though I would be in a hospital with staff around me. I spent the night at my sister's place and the next three weeks at my parents' farm.

The doctor recommended time off from work, which ended up being a total of three months. I spent the first few weeks at my parents' house in a drug-induced fog.

The sedative made me drowsy, so I slept a lot. It was nice to be able not to worry, and just to rest.

Still, the anxiety and worry were always there. When I was coherent, I worried about going back to work, being a burden, and if I would ever get better. I was also dealing with the feelings from the end of the relationship. Processing all of the negative things that he told me, trying to find a way out of the darkness, fighting to regain the knowledge that I am worth saving, I am worth loving.

Along with those haunting words from my ex, the anxiety and panic attacks made me believe that I was weak and crazy. It was like they fed off of his negativity and festered inside of me until I couldn't take it anymore and ended up in the ER.

All I wanted was to feel normal. To be relaxed, and happy. I didn't feel strong enough to be normal; a part of me always thought that I have these mental illnesses because I am a weak person. I didn't want to be known as the unstable one. The woman that people whisper about. I felt completely alone most of the time, which is very hard for others to understand. I've heard it all: "Just get over it." "Get control of yourself." "Why don't you just deal with it?" "Everyone has anxiety; it's not a big deal." "Anxiety Disorder is just an excuse people use to freak out."

Tough love doesn't work for me either; it makes me shut down and not feel safe confiding in the person who delivered it.

I suppose I've always worried. I even got the Worry Wart bead at grade 6 camp! I wasn't diagnosed with Generalized Anxiety Disorder until I was thirty, and last year at 37 diagnosed with Panic Attack Disorder and Mild Depression when I hit rock bottom. Of course, the anxiety didn't start with this latest relationship; it has its roots in my childhood.

The psychological abuse I endured from my grandma and dad and other family members caused me to feel that I wasn't worthy enough for love. In my constant worrying about what I was doing, trying to reach some false standard I'd set for being good enough, the anxiety was created.

Since then, I noticed that my anxiety would get intense when I wasn't in a healthy relationship. Of course, I didn't realize this until after the relationship was over, but now as I proceed with my life I know how to pay attention to those signs.

2016 was a rough year for me, but I have grown and changed so much since then. With the help of my family, friends, and psychiatrist, I was able to accept the anxiety and panic not fight it. Once I was able to say to myself, "Okay Martina, you are having an anxiety attack, but it's okay, it won't last, just allow yourself to feel anxious," the anxiety lessened, and I was able to breathe and get a handle on my out of control brain.

I spent quite a bit of time learning to enjoy myself, to be okay being alone. I journaled, pages and pages every day actually, processing how I was feeling. I find it a lot easier to sort through my feelings when I start to write, and if I'm lucky I can figure out why I'm feeling a certain way. It took almost a year for me to realize that I am okay being by myself. I learned not to put pressure on myself to be "perfect" or "normal," to be in a relationship.

Today I am only on my anxiety/depression pills. I went off of the sleeping pills two months after being prescribed them. They scared me, and, I didn't want to become reliant on them or accidentally mix medications and die in my sleep. After a year of being on the sedative, I also gradually reduced that dosage, and when I felt confident about myself, I stopped.

The sedative had affected my memory, and when I went back to work after three months, I had a hard time remembering things my boss told me. It was important for me to take the medications; they helped me to feel more stable and to get through each day.

In the past year, I've learned to be more open with my family and my boss about how I'm feeling. If I'm having a bad day at work, I can talk to my boss, explain what's going on and I can take time off. It is a huge relief to have a strong support system such as my family. To know that I can tell them when I'm having a bad day when I'm starting to feel the anxiety creeping closer to me and take steps to prepare for it. I accept that I am having an anxiety attack and I usually try to spend time with my sister, my niece or my mom.

I now can accept that I have anxiety, and I know that I can survive it. Accepting the feelings, I'm dealing with will help them to fade away faster. Every day is a challenge to be mindful of my thinking. It's like standing on the edge of the abyss and being able to calm myself down instead of falling headfirst into the darkness. Now I admit some days are way easier than other days.

Running, in particular, has been something that has helped me to feel better and stronger both physically and mentally. This year my sister and I are competing in trail running competitions. Even though I have had some panic attacks on the trail, she's right there encouraging me to keep going and I can focus on finishing. It's been such a thrill and sense of accomplishment to do something I always wanted to do but was so fearful to do it.

Running is something that I never imagined I would do. I was never a runner. Now when I can run further, it's a rush of adrenaline, my body is working in unison to conquer the hills. I am outside in nature, and I am running, free of all constraint, free of all worries. I am in control. I get such a great feeling of loving myself. Of honoring my body. It's a wonderful feeling.

Living with Generalized Anxiety Disorder, Panic Attack Disorder, and Mild Depression isn't easy. It's a constant battle. The good days are really good. I feel normal. The bad days can be either mild or horrific and leave me feeling weak and crazy. I have learned to accept the bad days and be secure in the knowledge that the bad days won't last forever.

Most importantly, I have learned to love myself. I am worthy of love, and that starts with loving and accepting myself. The anxiety may always be with me, lurking in the shadows but that's okay. I have tools to help me cope, like running. I feel like I am running strong towards my future not letting the anxiety and panic disorder hold me back.

BIO: *Martina Soderquist*

Martina Soderquist lives in Spruce Grove, Alberta and she works as an admin assistant in the Healthcare sector. She is a huge animal lover and currently has two cats, Mia and Phoebe, and two horses, Debit and Holly.

Animals have always been a part of her life and she is working towards owning an animal rescue/rehabilitation center where she can take senior animals and give them a loving home. Being involved in helping animals is something Martina has always been passionate about.

Martina's hobbies include trail running with her sister and her niece, traveling, hiking, spending time with her animals, playing ringette, snowboarding, basically being outdoors and of course spending time with family!

Sacred Hearts Rising

Sometimes You Have To Heal Yourself

By Holly Holmberg

*O*n Friday nights when everyone came home from the city, we always converged at the same bar to catch up. I was twenty-two and figuring out my next steps in life; I had served three years in the Canadian Navy and was reasonably confident in myself, but a ten-month marriage to a military sweetheart had ended six months earlier, I was ready for a new beginning.

That particular night, I found my friends, settled into my seat and swept the crowd to see who was home. I noticed a lovely ass; its owner bent over the pool table. I recognized him as a local guy I knew, seven years my senior, and I had taken a scuba class with his wife. It turned out that he had been sitting with my group before I arrived, and we reconnected.

With a pain-filled face, he shared that he had moved home from Calgary and was getting divorced. He described a marriage with a cheating, narcissistic ex-wife, who used him to settle into her new job, a new boyfriend and then dump him. As they had been high school sweethearts, he was devastated. He'd done everything for her during their seven years of marriage. I was horrified that someone could be so cruel to another person, and as a healer, I was hooked line and sinker.

As a kid I would bring home dying animals and try to heal them; I didn't always succeed and was devastated when they died. My father would say, "Holly honey, not all creatures can be healed. Sometimes we need to let them go and heal ourselves." Little did I know the foreshadowing of his wisdom.

Our romance started slow, but with me thinking he was all that and a side of fries, I patiently waited. On our first date he apologized for taking so long to get in touch; he was in a state of deep depression over his separation and unable to move forward. My gut instinct twitched, but I quickly brushed it aside and rationalized. Who wouldn't be upset over a broken marriage? I'd been crushed at mine. On our third date, he asked me to go steady, seeing no one but him. Again a red flag, but I agreed. Mister tall dark and handsome was a "dream come true." We moved quickly forward and were living together two weeks later.

My first encounter with his temper was a month into our living together. Exhausted from work I wanted to go to bed early, and he wanted to visit his parents.

Reluctantly agreeing to my staying home, he left. As I was preparing for bed, my mother called saying she needed me at the pub I helped her manage, so begrudgingly I went. To my surprise when I entered, my parents were sitting with my childhood friend and ex-boyfriend, a surprise visit for us all. Time flew as we reminisced about childhood and how his family was doing until I looked up to see my boyfriend standing there with a dark and angry look on his face. Introducing him made things worse: he made a snide remark about my being tired and said it was time to go home.

Once home he accused me of lying to go on a date with another guy, saying I was no better than his ex-wife. Stunned, I explained that I was not lying, but he wouldn't listen. That night I learned that my male friends needed his approval; I had poor judgment and couldn't see that men had ulterior motives. It was also the beginning of the alienation of my family. He felt my mother was manipulative and plotting, trying to replace him with a man of her choosing, one who would be more receptive to her plans for me.

Red flags popped up all over, but they always had a rational explanation, such as him telling me, I was young, spoiled and inconsiderate and would learn proper behavior. We became engaged after six months, marrying the following year. Small issues that were never a problem in previous relationships continued to arise. He had to teach me how to manage money, have better style in furniture, décor, and clothing and my friends were of questionable character. Also, according to him, my mother was meddlesome, instigating trouble in our marriage. When I argued this, he would use my past "transgressions" as proof of how she was manipulating me to do her will.

Before our marriage, we'd agreed that I would be a stay home mom and raise our children, rather than working and them in daycare. With our one year anniversary, we also celebrated the birth of our son. My husband had wanted a little girl to mold into the perfect young lady, but our little man quickly won his father's heart. He would be a third generation heavy equipment operator and carry on the family business.

I was a happy being a mom, but as a wife, I was never able to meet his expectations. He said I was lazy, allowed clutter to build up, didn't put laundry away fast enough, let dishes sit in the sink, and let the baby's toys lay around, plus the yard was neglected.

Thus most mornings, I would receive a lecture regarding my lack of commitment to our home, marriage and him: "If you loved me and were committed to our marriage, you would show it by having pride in our home and never allow it to look like a pigsty!"

Twenty to thirty minutes after he left for work, he would call apologizing. He was so stressed out with work and needed my help to keep things perfect at home so that at night he could relax and unwind, rather than having to do my chores. His OCD couldn't handle the disorganization; it was extra stress he didn't need. "Help me by keeping up your end of things, because there is no "I" in "team," was a common ending to our conversation, leaving me feeling broken and inadequate as a person.

My home management skills were not the only thing to come under attack. Business ideas, opportunities outside of the home, past hobbies, sports and military service were all met with, "Into everything, and doing nothing; you are unable to pick one thing and stick with it!"

Contact with my family declined further. He never forbade me to visit, but he stopped going. He didn't like my mother and how she was trying to run my life, and seriously questioned why I even bothered going. His family relationship was also strained, as he felt that his brothers were beneath him. Once, this escalated into a fight and ended with the RCMP coming to our door. He was arrested and charged with assault causing bodily harm, his court case ending with a criminal record, a fine and year probation plus anger management therapy. We had no further contact with his family until our daughter was born three and a half years later. Her birth and his job loss were the beginning of the end of our marriage, and the start of me questioning my sanity.

My husband was an oilfield consultant, confident in himself and his job; he never understood why the people he worked with were "useless, retarded and incompetent." Four months before our daughter's birth, he was fired.

He spiraled into deep depression and beat himself up. My attempts to cheer him up only left me broken hearted and angry, when he would retaliate back with, "You don't understand what it is like. You've never really worked, nor do you know what it takes to hold down a real job." When he took a foreman job with a local construction company, things escalated. With his truck phone forwarded to the house in the evenings, I was no longer allowed to answer our phone, since his boss would be pissed if he called and I answered.

Stress increased with his exhausting work schedule and long hours, causing him to lose interest in the family and me. I demanded too much from him wanting family time, intimacy and even sex. He just wanted to be able to relax on the couch, have some downtime and watch his golf: after all, he provided me with everything.

I was inept and ridiculed his behavior too much. I was broken, and my reaction to his moodiness was unacceptable. A doctor's appointment was scheduled for me; he felt I needed medication to "calm down."

As both the kids were in school, the doctor recommended a part-time job, rather than a sedative, to help break up my day. My husband disagreed and said a job was pointless, as I wouldn't earn enough to make it worthwhile and my time was better served at home keeping things up. He was in control of the money and provided all that we needed, with this negative response I slipped into deep despair.

My self-esteem crashed, and my accomplishments in the years prior held little value or importance. According to him, my military service was something only losers did because they couldn't make it in the real world; my equestrian and biathlon accomplishments were that of a spoiled child, allowing my mother to live vicariously through me. Hunting with my father was pointless, as the meat was gross and tags and fuel were money wasted. The strong independent woman I was before my marriage was slowly stripped away. After thirteen years, I could no longer be trusted to make decisions of any kind: it was amazing that I could still tie my shoes.

I lived with Dr. Jeckel and Mr. Hyde, never knowing when his mood swings would happen. In reality, it never mattered because nothing that the kids and I did was good enough. We would stress and scurry around like cockroaches in the light, trying to perfect things before he would come home from work. He being away was the only time that we could truly relax and be ourselves.

When I expressed our pain about his behavior, it was always met with,

"You and the children are my world. I would never hurt you, and would die without you!"

After a few years, a new consulting job took him away to work. Although it was a break from the daily drama, his nightly calls home were draining. His depression spiraled into deep lows, requiring long phone conversations convincing him that life was worth living and yes I did truly love him (although I was beginning to question this myself).

In November 2006, I confided about my marriage, the children's and my mental health and the behaviors of my husband with my oldest brother. Due to my husband's behavior, my brother felt it safest for the kids and me to go to the Camrose woman's shelter and apply for a restraining order against my husband. As an RCMP member, my brother didn't feel that the kids and I would be safe staying with my parents.

My courtesy call to let my husband know that the kids and I were safe, was met with screaming rage "How could you embarrass me so, come home now!" After two weeks at the shelter, some counseling and promises that he would change, we returned home. The first night home, I was cornered and told how angry I made him, that my leaving and the restraining order against him were embarrassing, and "don't do it again."

To avoid altercation I talked him down as I had done countless times before, and the next morning I returned to the woman's shelter with the children.

In December 2006, I found an apartment in Camrose for the kids and me, but our separation was short-lived as my husband quit his job and moved in. He was unable to work because my behavior caused his nervous breakdown.

June brought his return to work, school's end and our return home. Two months would pass before I was trusted to have a house key; the locks were changed while we were in the shelter.

From 2007 – 2010 in spite of marriage and personal counseling, our lives were fraught with arguing and discussion of divorce. Our counselor, being a fellow horseman recommended a personal growth book based on equine therapy for me to read. And my husband insisting that I get all the help I could, willingly bought the book for me.

This and three other books would guide me back to my true self, and help me establish a clear vision of the life I wished to live. Initially, I wrote a list of positive qualities that I wanted in my husband. But I soon realized that he would never change and that it was "I" who had to change to heal and guide my children to a better life.

In spring of 2010, I filed for divorce. His initial anger cooled when he came home with flowers and wine. The wine worked, along with promises of personal growth and change. Suspecting my husband was bipolar, hated women and was a narcissist (at least according to Google), the honeymoon lasted a week. Then a mutual friend pointed out the seduction plot (he got you drunk), and by this time I called it as I saw it—abuse.

In September 2010, I awoke one morning in a bitter, angry rage. My day hadn't even started. Who was this person I had become? I was everything that I didn't want to be, bitter about life and marriage. This was not the legacy I desired for my children. Within two weeks and keeping quiet so not to signal my escape, I found a home and furnished it with the basics. The Friday of the Thanksgiving long weekend my husband walked into our home. I told him that it was over and walked out, leaving him and the children behind. I had to get out and save myself, then save my children.

Crying, I arrived at my house; fear, pain, and relief flooded me, but the fight had just begun. My husband took control of the divorce proceedings with a collaborative divorce to keep me from getting "his" money, and to obtain joint custody of the kids. Things went quickly, but not smoothly, and I learned to stand up to his bullying.

Being unable to fight with me, he started verbally attacking our twelve-year-old daughter. Screaming matches between them ensued, damaging her mental health. When she was fifteen, my ex-husband physically beat "his princess." In the midst of this, he phoned me.

My blood ran cold, hearing her screaming for her life in the background. He screamed at her, "You are a whore, no better than your mother!" then screamed at me, "You turned her against me!"

Calmly talking him down, we agreed to meet at a half-way point for me to pick up our daughter.

I didn't know the depth of her injuries. Bruised ribs, concussion, and being choked until she was safely home. No charges were pressed since she was terrified to see or face him in court.

The ex-husband attempted suicide six months after beating our daughter, triggering a roller coaster of pain for us all. For two years my daughter was suicidal, and I never knew when I came home from work if depression and cutting would take her life.

This crash course in mental health has started the healing for our children. They ask, "Mom, why did you go back?"

My answer "I loved him and thought I could heal him, but Grandpa was right. Not all hurt creatures can be helped. Sometimes you have to let go and heal yourself."

BIO: *Holly Holmberg*

Holly Holmberg is a wild woman, farm girl, and independent soul.

Many experiences have shaped Holly into the multi-faceted woman she is today. Holly is and was: a survivor of child molestation, a temporary paraplegic, junior Canadian equestrian team qualifier, '88 Canadian Woman's Olympic Biathlon team short-list qualifier, one of the first woman on a Canadian Navy vessel in a war trade, and survivor of a twenty-year abusive marriage to an undiagnosed bi-polar partner.

A clinically trained holistic therapist, Holly's practice includes workshops and speaking on the multiple applications and clinical use of essential oils with animals and humans. With her new husband, Holly lives off-grid in the Alberta foothills, writing her book on the use of essential oils for everyday life applications, as well as divorce, sexual abuse, mental health, grief, and more.

Sacred Hearts Rising

Somewhere Over the Rainbow

By Laura-Lee Harrison

I held my baby boy on my chest, as my sister cried beside me telling me how beautiful he was and how proud of me she was. As my only support during labor, she was with me all night by my side, holding my hand and rubbing my back. Shortly after I had my beautiful, healthy boy, I was taken to my room to recover.

I was overcome with fear of being alone in the hospital after 8 pm as no one was allowed in my room except for the father. Now a single mother and in fear for our lives, I had to stay strong. The nurses knew not to share our information with anyone unless otherwise advised. I had a few visitors; then it was just me and this perfect little human.

To my surprise, as lonely, angry and sad I was that I was not sharing these astounding moments with a father type person or with my late mother, the joy that I created this human far exceeded my multitude of emotions. As I sang, "Somewhere Over the Rainbow" to my brand new baby as he lay on my chest, I vowed to create a healthy living environment for him, no matter what I had to do. This was my chance to change the cycles in my life.

I've cried a million tears for the loss of my mother and how unfair it is she is no longer here after she somehow found herself with Flesh-Eating Disease. Before my relationship with my son's father, for lack of better words, my mom and I were best friends. I told her everything and anything I didn't tell her, she knew somehow. When things went bad in my relationship, I stopped calling her as much. Her health was not the greatest, and I did not want to be the cause of any stress, making her more ill.

It was less than a month before she passed when I finally came clean to her about my relationship and that my partner was in jail and why he was there. It felt good to talk to my mother again like we used to, and I was looking forward to their visit to see me in Alberta. But that visit never happened. On the day they were to leave mom ended up in the hospital in British Columbia on life support.

Mom's illness was a surprise to us all, and all the turmoil surrounding her condition was devastating. Within a couple of days, my mom went from coming to seeing me to passing away, I was so heartbroken to realize that I didn't have my mom to talk to anymore and to make matters worse, I was riddled with guilt for burdening her with my problems.

I was mad at myself for years, and the guilt I had for burdening her took a very long time to let that guilty feeling go. I also agonize over the decision my family, and I made in taking her off life support in early 2013. A thousand questions ran through my mind, questioning everything we did for mom.

Would she have survived this horrible disease? Did we make the wrong decision?

Did the doctor wrongly diagnose her?

'Woulda,' 'coulda,' and 'what if,' plagued me for a long time. I often question if she could have survived.

To make matters worse for me, my mother always wanted a grandchild from me and was over the moon when I had told her I was pregnant for the first time in 2012. With the mounting pressure from my boyfriend, who was in jail at the time to get rid of the baby, I had an abortion. Instead of telling my mother that news I chose to tell her I had a miscarriage instead. I was not in a good place mentally and emotionally at the time, and my boyfriend was able to manipulate me into doing something I did not want to do at all.

I have wondered what if my baby was all she needed to be happy enough to overcome what had ultimately taken her away from me. The guilt of that decision controlled my life in many instances; it was like it had a power over me. Guilt is a very powerful emotion and robs you of your life if you let it. I am now in a space where I do not allow these thoughts to control me. I do not cry for days or hours anymore. I speak with my mother regularly and trust she is with us daily. I feel that my mom did get a grandchild to look after, just not in the physical sense.

When I was 25, I met the love of my life. We moved in together right away, and he was amazing. People that knew us always had wonderful things to say about us. Then little things started to happen, mild emotional abuse that I couldn't quite place. I thought it was normal and we went on with our life. After six months of being together, he went to jail. His jail time has nothing to do with me, the situation happened years before I knew him, and is not my story to tell, so I will not be sharing that within these pages.

I can say this; he had me convinced he was a good loving man and father. While he was away, he was nothing short of loving and supportive. Right after he was sentenced, I found out I was pregnant. I remember finally being able to speak with him on the phone. He was so excited for our baby. But the next call we had, he wasn't so excited and started planting seeds that I would be better off not having the child. During our conversations he had me convinced for our family's sake and his sake I should have an abortion. He could not stand the thought of me being a single mother or him not being part of our lives. He was such a smooth talker and made sense in his concerns for me and our baby that I started to believe he was right. I had my first abortion.

Unfortunately, with the use of an IUD for birth control, we found ourselves pregnant again after he was released from jail. This time the doctors had suggested it was possible it wouldn't be a viable pregnancy but had not determined that for sure. Before I could choose what I was to do, my boyfriend told me there was no way I was ever keeping that child. He repeated what the doctors had said, and drilled it into my head, "it wouldn't be a viable pregnancy." He refused to allow me to take actions to determine if I could have carried the child to term. I was forced to have my second abortion.

After my abortions, his awareness of me wanting a child, and the guilt I had over the abortions, he played on my emotional state and constantly told me that I should never think about having a child as I would be the world's worst mother ever to exist. He would use our puppy as his prime example, and would say that I couldn't properly take care of our puppy so how could I be a mother to a human.

These words that he drilled into my head about my worthiness, and ability to function as a responsible parent haunted me for years. It has taken many people in my life, old and new, telling me what an amazing mother I am currently, and what a smart, kind, loving young man I am raising my child to be. I am very proud to recognize I am an amazing mother, and I am raising an incredible little boy.

My purpose in sharing this is to open up light on abortion. Even though my choices were manipulated and not truly mine, I have still been judged and felt so ashamed that I felt that I needed to hide my truth. The abuse tactics that played a part in the manipulation and the forced decisions I made are also something I no longer hold on to and feel shame about.

I urge all women who have been faced with this decision to allow yourselves freedom from it. Whatever the reasons were, we do not need to feel shame or hide in the dark about decisions made because of domestic abuses. We must be kind to ourselves. I have learned to be kind to myself and forgive myself.

During my years with my ex-partner, I experienced not only manipulation and the two traumatizing abortions, but sexual, mental, physical, emotional and financial abuse.

When our relationship ended, if I spoke up about the abuse, people in our lives would not believe that he treated me in the ways he had. Some didn't believe me at all and shamed me for speaking out. Some I knew would never understand, so I decided to keep it to myself to protect myself.

After the breakup, I chose to partake in various forms therapies. The counselors were always shocked when I told them about my past, and now years later, I can see why.

I remember sitting and telling a counselor that my ex and I use to play fight. Harmless, right? Sure, until he would put me in a headlock with his arms or his legs, the "sleeper hold," and keep me in that position until I was on the brink of passing out. After the act, he would yell at me and blame me for almost passing out. This greatly concerned my counselors but I did not understand why. I thought he just didn't know his own strength, and got angry at me, as he felt bad for nearly killing me by suffocation.

My counselors were finally able to bring me to the light of what was happening and exactly how dangerous it was to be experiencing this type of physical abuse.

When I found out I was pregnant for the third time in 2014, he wanted me to have yet another abortion as he did not want a child, but I refused. With this refusal to bow down to his demands and manipulation he vowed that he would do whatever he could to have me have a miscarriage. Lying, cheating, alienation, scare tactics and harassment were all part of his schemes. He told mutual and multiple friends what he was going to do to me, to ensure I did not have my child. At one point his tactics almost worked as I ended up in the hospital bleeding during my second trimester.

My doctor advised me to quit my job, as we both worked at the same place of employment, where access to me was easy. Leaving me with no income before having a baby was a huge stressor, but I was determined to have this baby.

Once I had moved out of our place, on multiple occasions I woke up at 3 am hearing someone outside my house sneaking around, I knew it was him, but I had no proof. So nothing could be done to protect me, and he continued to do everything in a way I could not prove to the police that he was stalking me. I had hoped that since he was still on parole during this time that his parole officer could help, but I got nowhere again. Desperate and running out of options, I contacted the police again about what he was doing, but situations that are hearsay did not require any action. These disturbing events continued to happen until the birth of my child.

Approximately two months after my son was born I was diagnosed with chronic fatigue and a chronic pain disorder. I went to the doctor as picking up my young child caused me so much pain I would cry, and fatigue was so bad I was constantly worried I would drop him as I had no strength.

I have since struggled with weight gain, with addictive medications, with many types of excruciating pain, and with being so tired, I cannot do anything. Even lifting a finger was tiring some days. My doctors don't know definitively why I have this disorder. However, some research shows that trauma, and being in a state of fight or flight for extended periods of time, can be the cause of this condition. I believe this is why I experience my pain and fatigue. My body just could not process stress anymore.

After six years of many tears, fears, guilt, panic attacks, PTSD symptoms, much personal development, energy healing sessions, tapping sessions and gaining a whole new perspective on my life, I am pleased that I can say with confidence, I am blessed.

I was lucky to discover multiple ways of getting the professional support I needed during this time. I learned different techniques to stay grounded when a panic attack would present itself. I started to attend a woman's abuse group, which was pivotal in my learning and to my healing process. Hearing other women's stories week after week greatly helped me to realize, "It is not me." I did not do anything wrong. I just gave my heart to the wrong person, who took advantage of it.

There is nothing wrong with me as a human being, and I did not ask for this abuse. I also have the power to change my reaction to it, and no longer allow someone that power over me. I no longer experience panic attacks or PTSD Symptoms. My tears fall from my eyes a lot less. My guilt over my mother's death and my abortions are no longer a struggle. I have found my voice and my confidence. I choose to love freely and unconditionally. I do not need to fear pain. I am off all of my medications, and I experience very little pain if any at all. I am a strong single mother, and I am creating a life for my son and me to live with no limits.

If my story does anything, my sincere hope is that it allows someone to know that they too can survive whatever life has handed them. They too can overcome and see a lesson to build an abundant future.

BIO: *Laura-Lee Harrison*

Laura-Lee Harrison is a woman of many talents. As a mother of a two-year-old, she has her hands full! If that wasn't enough, she has an online health and wellness business, is a freelance makeup artist, special effects artist, esthetician, singer, energy healer, animal lover and an intuitive, Laura-Lee wears many shoes.

Committed to moving forward, her current efforts are focused on creating another company and a loving, fulfilled life for herself and her family.

In the Shadows

By Ahstyn Bigam

Divorce is a horrible thing to have to go through, especially if you are four years old. To this day, I'm still dealing with the aftermath of my parents' divorce. I've learned a lot from experience: how to calm myself down when someone is yelling, how to not let my stepbrothers get under my nerves, and many things that have helped me now and will help me in the future. Recently, things have been getting better. I've told my dad things that I could never tell him in the past, and my stepmom and I have bonded over the years. Things will continue to get better, I know, with time. But when my mom and dad first split up, it was hard.

I remember waking up to my mom lightly shaking me, saying, "Ahstyn, wake up. We're going to spend some time with auntie and uncle."

I rubbed my eyes, looked around my parents' bedroom and noticed a small black suitcase with my clothes as well as my mom's.

I remember her trembling as she picked me up, to get me dressed and to brush my teeth.

I could tell something was wrong.

As we finished packing the last of my things, my black cat Dooey ran up to me and rubbed up against my legs.

My mom told me to say goodbye, and I did, not knowing that it was going to be a very long time before I saw him again.

When we arrived at my auntie and uncle's, we unloaded everything and got settled in their spare bedroom. Then I went outside to play with the puppies.

That weekend, my mom, auntie and I went back to my house, and I got to see my dad. That whole day I played outside while my mom and auntie packed up the rest of our things with my dad helping and not saying very much.

I stayed with my dad that weekend, playing with the cats and dogs. My dad didn't do much of anything while I was there that weekend; he just sat at his place at the table and stared out the window.

When the weekend was over, my mom and auntie came to pick me up. I don't remember very much after that, but I do remember my dad yelling and cursing as I left.

When I was seven years old, my mom, auntie and I lived in a tiny one bedroom house outside of Alberta Beach, just us and a few animals.

I remember one evening my mom sat me down at the kitchen table and told me that she and my dad were no longer together. Even though I didn't see my dad that much, I had always thought that we were still just visiting my auntie.

I yelled at her and told her I hated her for taking me away from my animals, my friends, and my dad. I told her she had lied to me, and I made sure she knew I was mad at her, not knowing that she did it all for me.

After I learned that I could still see my animals and I could still see my dad, I came to forgive her. To this day, I still feel bad for getting so angry at her, but back then I didn't know the whole story.

During my first year of grade school, I was raised by my auntie and grandma, my mom working day and night to support us. I didn't think anything of it, but my mom was a wreck, blaming herself for not being around. I couldn't blame her; she didn't get to see her daughter go through her first year of school. When I finished grade one, we moved into my grandma's house which helped with the financial situation.

Things were starting to look up for us—we moved into a bigger house in Spruce Grove, and I finally started to make new friends. Until the end of grade four. My best friend had moved to Red Deer, my dad had a new girlfriend, and my mom had just gone through a nasty break up with her fiancé. We lived with my auntie (yet again) in a smaller house, barely able to fit three people. And I remember being scared to look out the window in case my mom's ex-fiancé was there.

Towards the start of grade five, my mom had met a new guy, and we got a better house. Things were great for a while until I met my stepmom's kids.

When I first met my stepmom, I was nervous, as any kid would be. But it was nice to have someone to look after my dad and to also to have someone I could talk to. For the first few times I met her, I noticed how happy she made my dad, the happiest I had seen him in some time. It was good, life was good, and then my dad introduced me to the boys, three boys, all of different ages. At first, it was weird, to have others kids my age around my dad. We would just sit around the green kids' table and play Lego, not talking, all just minding our own business.

As we got to know each other a bit better, we had tons of fun playing with Legos and playing hide-and-go-seek. When my stepmother and her boys moved into a new and bigger house, we had more room to play and run around.

71

I got to spend Christmas with my dad and the boys, and I finally got to meet the oldest boy, who had just started his last year in high school. It was a good visit until I asked my dad if I could use his phone to call my mom to say Merry Christmas. I flipped his phone open and saw a picture of him and my stepmom on their horses riding side by side. I started to cry but kept it quiet, so no one heard me. I felt left out and abandoned. I kept it to myself, not wanting to upset my dad and his happiness. I spent the rest of Christmas holidays waiting to come home.

The next year, I got news that my dad was going to move my stepmom and her boys to his house. I was happy, but I was also hiding how I felt, which was, dread. I had spent half of my childhood in that house, and I didn't want anybody but me and my dad there, but I kept my feelings to myself.

When they moved into the house, the boys made my dad very angry and made him yell a lot, which scared me. I had seen my dad yell and get angry before, but never like that.

The youngest boy had moved into my old bedroom, kicking me out into the basement, which didn't help the feeling of being abandoned. Whenever my dad would get mad, I would go downstairs to my room and cry. I had to learn that if you did everything perfectly, you would not get yelled at. My days spent there were fear-filled, with many tearful periods of sleep. The boys had no regard for my personal things, and the boys and their friends would go into my room (which had no walls) and take things and wreck things. I didn't dare to tell my dad, for fear he would yell at me.

It got so bad that I would have panic attacks weeks before I had to go up there. I'm an only child, so I'm used to being around adults and not having other kids around. When I would go up, my dad would make me play with the others kids, which I hated. The only relief I got when going up there was seeing my grandparents and my auntie.

My stepmom would leave the discipline to my dad, which was unfair to him, having to look after someone else's kids. Everything changed when the boys went up to their dad's. It was like someone strange had taken over my dad's body; he was smiling and laughing and was happy. Until they came home.

After a while, when my dad became sick from blood clots, I was hysterical. I didn't know if he was going to die or live or anything, so being fed up with everything that was going on with my dad and the boys, I finally got enough courage to tell him I didn't want to come up to his house anymore. He wasn't mad or yelling, and the next day I went back home. And the next month I went back up to his place. He had ignored my request not to go up there anymore.

When I turned twelve, I didn't get a party or a happy birthday from my dad. Nothing. The youngest boy (whose birthday is a month after mine) got a party, presents and everything, even a happy birthday from my dad. That did not go over very well with me.

As the years went by I learned how to deal with the boys and my dad's anger. I still get panic attacks just thinking about going up there, but I learned how to talk myself through it.

One time when I had just turned thirteen, I went up there for two weeks. It started off just like all the other visits, and the oldest boy had come down from High Level to see his mom. Also, my dad had hired a new farm hand to help with the pasture. It rained almost every night and day, meaning we didn't have to go outside very much.

My dad and the farmhand worked early mornings, so I didn't have to worry about my dad yelling, which I liked. The oldest boy coming for a visit was also a good surprise since he could look after the boys, so I didn't have to. I got to spend two nights at my grandpa's, which is always fun, and when I got back to my dad's house, I found out that the boys had to go to their dad's house. My insides did a happy dance. When we dropped them off, my dad changed. He was smiling and laughing, which he rarely did, and it was a fun trip.

Usually, panic attacks would happen about four to five days before I would go up to see them, and it got so bad that some nights I would just wish my dad to die, so I wouldn't have to go through all of the hate and the stress. But the feeling of being at my dad's has slowly gotten better.

Most of the time, I'm no longer afraid to go up to see them, but sometimes all the feelings of fear and hate come back. Using the technique of telling myself how many days I have left until I go home is helping, and if the fear feeling gets bad, I go downstairs to my room and draw how I feel!

My sister Jaidin, who died before I was born, also had a big part in the release of all the stress. In butterfly form, she would visit me every day before I would leave to my dad's, then she would follow me everywhere, helping me deal with the stress and the fear during this time.

I believe that my dad's anger comes from my sister's passing. He won't acknowledge that she is no longer with us and he won't acknowledge that she ever existed. Whenever I try to bring up the subject of Jaidin, he quickly shuts me down. Since he was the carrier for the disease she was born with, I know he blames himself for my sister's passing.

He tries to be a good dad, but his anger is the main reason I don't want to see him. Also, if I want to check cows with him or anything just the two of us, my stepbrothers always come with us, so I never really get quality time with him.

Still, as I've gotten older, my dad has started to treat me as an adult, and as his daughter. I will never get over the fear of going up to see him, but learning to control my fear has gotten me more confident. Now I can finally tell him things I've wanted to tell him for a long time, like that I would like to spend Christmas with my mom, and that I would like to see him on specific days.

I love my dad, and that will never change, and hopefully, someday he will change for the better.

BIO: *Ahstyn Bigam*

Ahstyn lives in a small community outside of Edmonton, Alberta with her mother and Joey. She enjoys playing with her goats and her cat Mocha.

Sacred Hearts Rising

A Journey to Freedom

By Jannet Talbott

*O*n June 16, 2006, I was woken up by loud banging on the front door. I looked over at the clock on the nightstand; it was 4 am.

Who could it possibly be at this hour? My husband was out of town on business. He must have finished up early and flew home, and forgot his house key.

I got to the front door, squinting as I turned on the front entrance light. When I opened the door, there stood two uniformed police officers, one female, and the other male.

They asked me if they could come in and sit down, I was puzzled. I couldn't imagine what was so urgent that they came to my home at this hour. The male officer quickly revealed that they'd come to notify me that my brother, Jason, was deceased. That he hanged himself in the garage of my rental property where he lived.

I felt like the wind had been knocked out of me, my head was spinning. I was in complete disbelief at what the officer just told me, so I kept asking him if he was certain it was Jason. He assured me that it was. At that moment, the world stopped turning; I could physically feel my heart breaking and deep inside I knew that my life would never be the same again.

Jason was five years younger than me, and we'd had a close relationship his entire life. He was my absolute favorite person on the planet. I had always felt responsible for him, and I was there for him whenever he needed me. Before his death, I hadn't realized that he was also the person who tethered me to the planet.

At that time, I was in an unhealthy and abusive marriage, which I was too afraid to leave.

Days after Jason's funeral, I was reprimanded by my husband if he found me crying in the shower, or crying in our bedroom while watching the DVD my family had made of Jason's life, for his funeral. For my own self-preservation, I had to keep my grief bottled up inside of me, but something in me had changed.

Completely empty inside, I felt like I was the walking dead, I didn't have my usual radar up, walking on eggshells around my husband, which was my normal behavior.

Now, I just didn't care, I was completely untethered, like a lost soul. I wished someone would just push me in front of a moving bus.

On November 16, 2006, of that same year, my husband called me from his cell phone while driving. He said that he'd discovered I had left out a small detail from my accounts of the previous day. He was in the habit of tracking my daily movements, and he didn't like it if something was amiss. His voice got angrier, and I knew he was headed home and what that meant, so I hung up the phone grabbed the car keys and started driving. He pulled up behind me just as I was leaving our neighborhood. I could see from my rear view mirror that he was furious, motioning for me to pull over.

I drove until I could find a busy parking lot. He pulled up next to me, screaming through his open window, as he had pulled up too close to my vehicle so he couldn't open his car door to get out.

As I sat there looking at this frantic man, listening to him ramble on, I had a moment of clarity. I realized I no longer feared him, nor feared to leave him. I was more afraid of what would become of me if I didn't leave him. Even though I was mentally and emotionally exhausted and felt completely depleted, I knew I had to find the strength to take the next step and leave my husband.

The day I moved out of our marital home, my husband was supposed to be out of town on business, but I saw him parked up the street. There was no reason for him to be there as we had agreed that I would only take what I came into the marriage with, as well as a living room shelving unit.

I moved in with a girlfriend I knew from school who I had recently reconnected with. My husband didn't know her well, or where she lived, so this gave me time to think while I started the divorce proceedings. Since all I asked for was three months support, it was a quick and amicable divorce. I just wanted to get back on my feet and move back into my rental house. After staying with my girlfriend for a few weeks and with the divorce agreement in place, I moved in with my sister and her family, staying in their spare room in the basement.

At the same time, I was renovating my rental house with money I was able to take from the equity I had built up. I was forty years old, and I didn't know who I really was, what made me happy, or what my beliefs were. I didn't have a job or a vehicle of my own; all I had was my rental house which I purchased before meeting and marrying my husband. I let go of a great job with a U.S. company, to be a homemaker, and had sold my car when we moved to California for a year
with my husband's company.

I realized I had lived my entire life trying to make other people happy and had lost myself in the process. I was still grieving over the loss of Jason and trying to figure out how my life would be without him in it, or if I even wanted my life to continue.

Despite the bleakness I was feeling, I felt I had to take this time to figure a few things out, and also take responsibility for staying in my unhealthy marriage and allowing someone to treat me the way I had been treated.

Around this time, I started reading The Law of Attraction, by Esther and Jerry Hicks. It was my turning point, and that book may have saved my life. I started to go through the process of getting rid of beliefs that weren't mine, beliefs that were put on me from the time I was born, other people's beliefs that I had spent my whole life trying to live by.

As I started the lengthy and humbling process of peeling back the layers of whom I was and the things that made me happy, I discovered my own belief system. This was a pinnacle moment in my life, one that I would build on. No longer did I feel it was my job or responsibility to make other people happy. Especially at my own expense.

As I shifted my perspective and beliefs, people started coming into my life, people who helped me to heal on many levels. I started going for hypnotherapy to work through the aftermath of being in an abusive relationship, as well as the guilt I felt after Jason's suicide. I had allowed Jason's choice to take his own life, become a personal failure of mine, and to come to terms with that not being the case, took some time.

I was also introduced to people who have these amazing gifts to connect with those who have crossed-over. They gave me some incredible messages from Jason; they told me things only he and I would know.

Receiving these messages from Jason and messages from my Spirit Guides, comforted me and helped me to understand that there's more to life than what we see in front of us.

At this time, I was also acutely aware that I probably wouldn't be going through this incredible journey of discovery, if I hadn't lost the most important person in my life. Jason's sudden and unexpected death shook me to my core and put me on the ground floor. I found the courage to look at myself and to change the blueprint of my life. Jason was such a wonderful gift in my life, from the moment he was born; I will always cherish the memories I have of his time here on earth. When I see heart shapes anywhere, in rocks or leaves or even coffee grounds, I know that's his way of letting me know he's always with me.

I also found healing through animals. From the time I was a child, I'd always had pets, and while I was still renovating my house and living with my sister and her family, I started looking online at different breeds of dogs. One day I saw an ad for Golden-doodle puppies that were due to be born any day. I excitedly submitted my adoption application.

The puppies were two weeks old when I went to meet them and choose my puppy. I held up a couple of puppies and looked into their eyes, they both looked away, then I held up this one male puppy, and when I looked into his eyes, he didn't look away. Instead, he looked at me as if to say, "It's me you should choose. It's me who will take care of you."

And he did, for ten glorious years. He passed away in July of 2017 from hemangiosarcoma. I named him Riley, and picked him up six weeks later, the day after I moved back into my renovated rental house. We were inseparable and went everywhere together. Riley would ride in the crew cab of my truck with his head out the window, ears flapping in the wind, and I would watch people smile at him as they drove past us. He loved it. He loved people, he loved life, and mostly, he loved me. Riley was such a blessing in my life; he helped me to feel joy again, to laugh again and to love again.

I continued to utilize the teachings of The Law of Attraction, and I learned that I could manifest whatever it was that I wanted to attract into my life, and I also learned that whatever I was focusing on, good or bad, I was attracting to me. During my daily fifteen-minute manifesting session, I started manifesting my future ranch, which eventually I would name the Double J Freedom Ranch, in honor of Jason and our life together and I feel Jason found freedom from his personal suffering on earth, and me finding freedom in choosing a different life path. This ranch would be my legacy; it would be freedom for those who lived there or visited, and also a place of healing.

Fast forward eleven years. So much has come to pass. I developed an all-natural pet supplement which has been on the market since 2006, my company is called, Riley's Legacy Inc. and I acquired my 160-acre farm property in 2015. I'm currently working to raise money to finance my next venture, to build a barn aptly named, The Healing Barn, with an attached indoor riding arena. This facility will be for equine owners to bring their sick or injured horses to receive daily care and treatment until they're well enough to return home.

Through my first Mexican rescue dog Wilson, who I adopted in June of 2011, I learned about the suffering and cruelty that happens to dogs in some countries. During the past five years, I've helped the dogs in Mexico any way I can, whether I'm flying down donations, medical supplies, and dog crates, volunteering at spay and neuter clinics, flying down to bring adopted dogs back or finding loving forever homes for dogs in Canada and the US. To teach children to be compassionate towards animals, I'll be self-publishing a children's book telling Wilson's story of his life on the street.

Eleven years ago, that night when those police officers knocked on my door, I never could have imagined how my life would change or where it would lead me. I couldn't have imagined how free I would feel, and how I would become my true authentic self. How every morning I walk out the front door of the Double J Freedom Ranch and see my horses waiting for me by the fence for their morning feed, and the smell of the morning dew, and watching my dogs happily running free around the yard while I make my way over to the horses. How I go out into the pasture to bring in my mare, taking my time while brushing her out before I saddle her up for a ride in my hay field. With nothing but gratitude in my heart as the sun shines down on my face, and the wind blows through my hair when my mare goes into a smooth gallop, feeling pure and joyous freedom.

BIO: *Jannet Talbott*

From the time Jannet Talbott could walk and talk, she was bringing any and all living creatures into the house for shelter, food and love. This love for animals has stayed with her, and helping animals has become her passion and chosen profession.

Jannet developed an all-natural pet supplement, which has been on the market since 2006. She also travels to Mexico to volunteer with Spay and Neuter clinics, transports medical supplies, donations, and dog crates, and flies dogs back to Edmonton to place them in loving forever homes.

Her dream of living on her own ranch came true in 2015 when she acquired her farm on a quarter section of land near the town of Barrhead, Alberta, where she now has many dogs, cats and horses. Jannet's next project is raising money to build "The Healing Barn," a barn with an attached indoor riding arena, to hand walk and exercise horses that need daily care as they recover from injuries.

Jannet has named her farm the Double J Freedom Ranch, which has been more hard work and more amazing than she could have ever imagined.

Opening the Invisible Drawer

By Thyra Whitford

*A*lthough I was the baby of my family, when I was born, Mom and Dad hadn't quite figured out how to do the whole "stable parent" game. Childhood memories consist of living in a series of dilapidated locations that let nature in, some with no indoor plumbing, plenty of midnight moves, frequent school changes, torrid fights between parents, parties with strange people landing in our beds, and recurrent stays in vehicles outside a series of bars. A recipe certain to produce plump, and juicy repressed memories.

Through my experience of healing from trauma, I have learned that the human mind is an amazing blessing for us. It protects us as nothing else can. The mind takes the event, wraps it in its entirety, and places it carefully in a drawer, lined with an impermeable layer and locked with a seemingly invisible key. The lock is hidden, the drawer is hidden, and we get on with life. It houses the memories in completion, safe and secure, until we are strong enough and with enough tools around us, to make sense of them. Even if we attempt to force ourselves to remember, the mind will only release the package when the timeline is right to do so.

The series of events that opened my last repressed memory perfectly illustrates this release.

Nine years ago, I dated a doctor for a spell. He was handsome and successful. Several weeks had passed, with us dating a few times a week before the first kiss. Soon after, our telephone conversations began to include his bedroom suggestions. I wasn't sure I was ready for the next step with him, but I didn't want to give up just yet. I could feel something was "off," but perhaps it was just me being too sensitive?

I knew there were at least two factors making me uncomfortable.

One: I take my time with relationships as I was date raped by a young realtor when I was 20. Since then, if the guy is too pushy, that's my sign to walk away. But I ignored my instincts. This guy was a doctor. I could trust him, couldn't I?

And two: We frequented some of the same circles, and I witnessed the doctor swooning over another lady, yet he continued to call me. Yup, the signs were there, but something still drew me to him.

On Halloween, I used the holiday to invite the doctor over for supper, to hand out candy, and to talk. I felt I had gotten to know him well enough to have the date at my house.

Right after supper, he shifted the conversation to the bedroom, and I used that as an intro to talk about what I had seen with him and the other woman. After a few minutes of denial, he shared that he had slept with the gal, but, of course, "it wasn't serious." Warning bells and buzzers were already going off inside me. I could see now that he was playing me, and here he was, in my house. Just me and him. How could I, of all people, let that happen?

Very shortly after, he made his move. I spent the next few minutes protecting myself and trying to find kind ways to say "no." These attempts were useless; however, what was fascinating was where my mind went in those next few minutes.

I heard a voice in my head clearly say, "You're not safe! Just let him do it, then it can be over, he can leave, and you can live and get on with your life!"

Memories flashed in my mind back to the rape when I was 20. Those same words had surfaced at that time as well.

I remembered an experience after that - how a welder I was in a relationship with wanted to explore more in the bedroom. I had to admit my rape experience to explain my resistance. Oddly, the welder became very adamant that if I would have just said "no," it wouldn't have happened. Well, I did say "no," but my inside language was saying "no" was an unsafe word. Why?

All these thoughts while my body was going through the motions of attempting to deny the doctor's persistence to have his way.

Then I remembered how long it took to get over the date rape, and how just letting it happen wasn't worth it. Nothing was worse than that. And that was it. Right there and then, on my Halloween date that had turned so sour, I made up my mind. The answer was "no."

By that point the good doctor had me pinned against a wall and was maneuvering to pull me upstairs to my bedroom.

Calm words came from me as I looked directly at him. "This is not going to happen." He backed up a bit, and then defiantly said, "You bet it is!"

At that moment, a sense of peace came over me. I knew it wasn't going to happen. I knew I had all the power. I felt like I was 600 pounds of solid lead. I was immovable. I stood still, and quiet as he attempted to lift me.

"This is not going to happen," I heard myself repeat. Again, so very calm. A few more tries and I heard from him, "I guess I better go." "I guess you better," came out of me. And, off he went.

Who had been talking? My voice. My body. But, was that me?

Something came over me. Empowerment. I knew, without a shadow of a doubt, that type of situation would never happen to me again. This was my first ah-ha of many.

I believe that everything happens for a Divine reason, and all events have the capacity to make us better, stronger, and wiser. To me, true forgiveness is a feeling of overwhelming gratitude for the challenging events that occurred. Today I remain so grateful to the good doctor. Without that interaction, I may have never found my way to this strength. I saw him years later at a church event and even hugged him. No shaking. Nothing but power. That said, something continued to haunt me. My internal language of "Just let it happen so you can live." Where did that come from?

In the years that followed, I knew I had more to explore. I had not forgiven the young realtor. Although I knew it would never happen again, I still found it difficult to look at those memories. I couldn't spend enough time in it to find the value or gratitude. There was something more for me to learn, but what?

Now I had the precious self-talk to focus on. Why did I feel it was unsafe to say "no" to the realtor? Why did I need just to allow him to "get it over with?" Did I believe that he was going to physically harm me if I didn't comply? Well, the truth is, I didn't know. I just knew that me saying "no" wasn't working.

What about the comments from my welder? Was he onto something? If I would have said "no" in another way, would everything be different?

For about five years, these thoughts and questions would arise without warning, and never seem to have a solution, so I would stuff them back into the drawer. That impermeable lining was turning into paper. Easier to access, but not completely. It was now a place that was never secure enough to stay closed but could be out of sight for a moment so I could carry on.

Sometime within that fifth year, the questions were replaced with something different. Snippets of memories. A specific memory of when I was a very young girl. Mom and Dad had gone to the bar, and this time they left me with an older couple. I didn't know them. I remembered him bouncing me on his knee, too close to his body. I felt uncomfortable. Then, nothing. Over and over that incomplete memory persisted.

For the best part of the next year, the partial memory would dart in and out without warning. Always the same. Though I would sit quietly with it each time, asking, and sometimes begging, to see the rest of the story, my pleas were not answered. I became impatient. I told myself "I'm an adult. I can be proactive, and get to the bottom of this."

I have a good friend who is skilled in past life regression. We made an appointment, and she sat with me as I took my time to ease into the process. I was ready to see the whole picture, or so I thought.

A story unfurled in front of my eyes that seemed so incredibly unreal. Like a movie. I felt no emotion, and my new self-talk was deflating. "How could anyone do such things to a child? If it really happened, surely I would have remembered, right? Maybe it was just my imagination."

When the session was over, I put it all back in the drawer. It wasn't true, and if it was, there was no proof, and I couldn't remember it, so it no longer mattered. "Get on with your life," were the words that came. "You're okay."

Over the next year or so, occasionally the drawer would open, and I would see the old pictures, and sometimes the new ones from my session with my friend. The new memories had no emotion tied to them at all. "No matter, what can I do about it anyways press on."

About a year and a half ago I connected with the love of my life. We had dated on and off through the years, but this time was different. We were both ready for each other. Though this union was loving and magical, there was a spell of time where I just couldn't find happiness. Everything set me off. I had no filter to sort out what was worth getting upset about.

Through it all, my love stood strong. I was certain several times that he would leave. He continuously let me find my way back to him. Finally, I got to the place where I decided I would not leave.

It was in that feeling of safety when something happened. Vivid memories of me as a girl revealed themselves. I saw and felt the whole experience like I was there. It was graphic and horrifying. I saw what happened to me and how I got out. I saw how strong I was even as a child, and how much help I had from what I think was the other side. I could see, feel, smell, taste and hear everything. There was no denying it now. It happened.

I was shown the situation in a time where I felt safe and had enough tools and love around me that I could manage the emotion, and make sense of it. My Love held the key to my invisible drawer.

Aside from the first day of the vivid memories, it was not like reliving it. It was more like therapy and a series of ah-ha's. Pictures of the event involuntarily played over and over until I was desensitized. Until I could see beyond the fear.

This new revelation explained why I had those thoughts with the young realtor. There were similarities to the event when I was a girl, and in that situation, to resist was to die. Ah-ha! I am so grateful to him now. That event was pivotal in unraveling the mystery of my last repressed memory.

Knowledge of this childhood event explained why my welder felt the need to share his opinion so strongly with me. The entire experience showed me how to stand up and say "no" with my whole being, and what power that brings! Ah-ha! Thank-you to the realtor, and again to the doctor, for playing his part.

As I believe we choose our parents and families, this experience has also explained why I would choose to come to them in this lifetime. In their seemingly self-absorbed ways, they let me slip through the normal parenting securities, (such as; don't leave your children with strangers), and I had to experience it in its entirety so that I could learn. I am so grateful to each of them!

Knowing what happened explained so many things about why I do the things I do. My hurdles and self-sabotaging behaviors, and my strengths and successes. Once I knew the "why's" I had the power. I could decide to change or keep things the same.

I continue to learn from this revealed childhood memory and to be amazed by the human mind, and journey, and that an event appearing catastrophically horrifying could also have a side so incredibly positive and uplifting. This event in my past is the reason I feel so compelled to assist humanity wherever I am called. It made me strong, independent and able to mediate and help people find the best in themselves again.

I know there is more to learn, as that is the purpose. I allow the complete memory to become a part of my fabric. That thin and seemingly fragile thread when alone is now invited to entwine with love, and the rest of me, to become a powerful conduit for wisdom and strength.

BIO: *Thyra Whitford*

Thyra Whitford is an artist, author, and energy healer. As an energy healer, she has training in Reiki and Multi-reflexology, and utilizes her natural gifts as an empath, intuitive, clairsentient, and clairaudient, to assist others in better understanding the messages of the body, and life-path journeys.

She offers private and confidential sessions, as well as group courses for other empaths and those interested in discovering and exploring their own gifts.

Thyra's first book was A Reference Guide for Empaths, and she's in the process of completing a children's book about the value of recycling, as well as a series of novels that describe many of the spiritual happenings she has been privy to during her time as a healer.

Thyra sold her first piece of art in 1995, and many pieces since. Her media varies from wildlife realism in oils, to portraits and nature in acrylics, sculpting and sculpting on canvas, illustrations for logos, signs, and books, as well as drawings, paintings and canvas sculptures of the Divine Guides and Guardians that walk with us, as she sees them.

Thyra Whitford, RMP, MRT twhitford@shaw.ca
www.thyrawhitford.com

The Broken Porcelain Doll

By Elizabeth J.O. Gagnon

When I was little, one bright spot for me was seeing my great grandma. We didn't visit her very often, but to me, she was a hero who helped me feel special at a time when I had so much darkness around me. I remember her sharing with me the story of having her first cup of tea when she immigrated to Canada from Germany during the Hitler years. Her message to me was: take time for tea, reflect on where you want to go in life, and set your goals and dreams with a full heart in everything you do.

Most of all, she said, enjoy the flavor of the tea as you drink it and take it as a drink of strength to go on.

Now I do all that she suggested when I settle in by myself with a cup of tea. I also use my teatime alone to talk to loved ones, like my great grandma, who has passed. I have a sit down with them in spirit. And I love hosting tea parties, to give others a chance to share their stories of strength and inspiration through sharing a cup of tea. At every party, I also share my great grandma's words.

It's important to me that people's stories are heard because I know what it's like to be silenced.

I was born a reddish-blonde curly haired girl in a Northern Ontario town named Hearst. I was shy and soft-spoken, a delicate child. Now I think of myself back then, as a porcelain doll, a girl who should have been handled with care and love. But at the age of four, my life changed forever, with the first crack in my porcelain body. Cracking that would soon become the everyday breaking down of the little girl I was.

On my fourth birthday, after everyone had gone to bed, my uncle woke me up and said he had another birthday gift for me. Since I was so young, at first, the idea of another present seemed like a good thing

It's hard to express how fast my spirit went out that night. With anger, my uncle grabbed my arm, and I followed him into the bathroom. He stuffed his old dirty hanky in my mouth, making me gag. He whispered in my ear, "Stay quiet." I started to cry in fear which made him grab my arm tighter, and he forced me to my hands and knees. He asked, "Don't you want your present?" I wondered what could be in there for me to have. I was still crying and asking to go back to my bed, but instead, he said it was time for me to become a big girl now.

Needless to say, I hated his present. After he raped me, he told me to go back to bed like a good little girl. He sneered. "If you say anything, you will be in big, big trouble and everyone will hate you."

Those words would stay stuck in my head for many, many years.

The next morning I woke up black and blue all over and tried to cover the bruises up with a jogging suit. My mother caught me, looked at my clothes from the night before, and accused me of wetting myself.

"No," I said, but before I could tell her the truth my uncle rounded the corner and glared at me to silence me.

I was punished for wetting myself, which left me confused, and my grandma gave me a huge red pill for a non-existent bladder problem. From that night on and for many more years my uncle would continue to give me what he called his "big girl presents."

I believe that Mom knew but drew a blind eye. She wasn't there much for us kids growing up and would be gone for days at a time. Lots of our time was spent with other family and foster homes. One night at my Aunt's, my mom and I were sleeping on a mattress on the floor when my uncle came in. When he got on top of me, Mom turned over and looked me in the eyes as if to ask, "What do I do?" Doing nothing to stop the abuse from my uncle, she rolled over and pretended to be asleep while he continued.

The next morning my mom looked at me like I was garbage. She said I was smelly and that I should wash.

When I was ten, I remember asking my mom, "What would you do if someone was touching my bum?" I was told to stop lying and being crazy. Then I asked her how she would help me, which made her upset and changed the subject. I felt like she knew, but didn't want to hear it.

So many years of abuse took place that I felt like the only way this would stop would be if I died. At age twelve, I was in school, and this young boy who had a crush on me asked if I'd be his girlfriend. I said no. I already had two so-called boyfriends, I knew what they did, and I didn't want that anymore.

My godfather was my second abuser, and way worse than my uncle ever was. He would wait until my godmother went to work before showing me what a big girl was.

He'd lock his son and his stepsons in the room next to his. Then I was told to sit on the couch so he and I could play a game. I told him I didn't feel well and didn't want to play. I tried to run for the door, but he grabbed me by my arm and dragged me into his bedroom. He told me I was taking the fun out of the game.

I screamed as he pulled me into his room and threw me on the bed.

All I wanted to do was go home. I yelled louder telling him to leave me alone, as the boys in the other room banged on the wall telling him to leave me alone.

He yelled at the boys to shut up or, they'd get what was coming to them. I'll never forget the words he whispered in my ear: "Love hurts."

When he was finally done, he said that he'd kill me if I ever told the secret. I hated him and his game. I lived in fear, for something he did to me. New cracks in my porcelain body every time. He raped me three more times when I was forced to go to my godparent's house. When I protested going back there, my mother told that I'd be punished if I didn't go because I needed to learn religion from them.

At an early age, I did as I was told, even if I didn't want too.

One day at school, I was pulled aside by a teacher to answer a few questions, which resulted in the police and CAS being called. At the police station, my mom joined me. Privately she told me I better not be lying or making trouble, but when the police were in the room and spoke about how I'd been abused, she acted upset.

I learned that the two men who had shattered my body and spirit would be going to court, and I'd have to face them. Nine years of abuse equaled nine months of prison time for my uncle, who served only six for "good behavior." My godfather only did three weekends, had to pay a fine, and was given a restraining order.

I don't understand the legal system.

Upon my uncles' release from prison, he was greeted with a big celebration. Seen as a troublemaker, I was left locked at home alone while everyone else attended it. Why was I being punished for something that wasn't my fault?

Wanting to be with my siblings, I went to the party on my own to act like nothing happened.

Since no one in my family believed me, my uncle resumed his abuse. This time I got pregnant, and still, no one believed me. My baby was stillborn at five and a half months. I was able to name her but was to never speak of her again. When I mentioned her, my parents threatened to send me away or lock me up again. That's how they kept the family secrets hidden.

At fourteen years old, I developed an eating disorder to cope with losing my daughter.

When I was seventeen, I got pregnant again, this time by my boyfriend. My father threatened to have the baby taken from me or that he'd disown me for having a baby out of wedlock if I didn't get married.

On my wedding day, my father's last words to me were, "Where're my two bucks? Once I get my money, then he can have you." Apparently, that was the agreement with my soon to be husband. I felt like a whore being sent off. I always hated my wedding day because it was full of abuse and disgust instead of joy and excitement.

I was married for sixteen long years, and the cycle of abuse continued for me—physically, sexually, mentally, financially and emotionally.

No matter what happened, no one ever listened. I felt let down by family, friends, and the community. I slowly just shut everyone out. I became someone I no longer knew; I became who they wanted—not a real person, but a doll, a thing to be used and abused.

The only good to come out of any of that was my four children. I honestly believe I get my strength from them. Because of them, I found the courage to get a divorce and to say I needed some help. I got a full- time job and found a place to start fresh, trying to be the perfect mom. In the end, it proved to be too much. My body shut down, and I ended up in the hospital.

I had a physical and mental breakdown and needed rest. My youngest daughter's godparents offered to help until I was better. During my hospital stay, however, they gave notice to my landlord, moved my belongings to their home and gave some to my ex-husband.

When I left the hospital, I had no place to live or raise my kids. I turned to my family for help and was told, "Figure it out on your own."

Thinking it was the right choice, I released my children into foster homes I picked for them. As my strength grew, I wanted my children back, but they asked me to leave them where they were. Understanding what it felt like to be not heard and wanting my children to feel like I heard them, I signed over my parental rights to the foster families.

It took me two months to sign, as it was the hardest decision I would ever make, knowing I'd never have my kids again.

Every day I regret that decision. Due to distance, lack of communication and court rulings not followed by their foster parents and CAS, my relationship with my children has suffered to this day. Every day, I also know that in deciding to sign those papers and protect my children, I stopped the cycle of sexual abuse for them. For that, I am thankful.

For most of my life, I was confused and wondered why me? I was the broken doll everyone would use and abuse anytime they wanted and then say, "Oh she's crazy; she needs help." To me, they were the ones who needed the help.

For many years, I kept the peace and lived with the cracks in myself, until I moved away. I realized that I don't need them in my life and I can go on without them. I've been called many names, told "let it go to God" or "forgive him; he's done his time." The latest one I've heard from family members: "I doubt he did any of that to you: you're just a troublemaker." It makes me want to scream.

I believe they're all sick and don't, or don't want to see the damage they did to me. In my forties, I still fear some of my family, which is one of the reasons I avoid going back home. As no one has ever protected me, I have no faith in my family.

Due to years of abuse, I suffer from C-PTSD, Conversion, Dissociation, Borderline Personality, Identity and Eating Disorders. But I'm no longer that broken porcelain doll. Since my father died and I no longer fear him, I'm finally able to grieve for my lost daughter, and I'm taking other steps to take care of myself.

To help me deal with and overcome my past traumas, I started Miss Liz Tea Parties, events where I invite others to speak and share their stories over a cup of tea.

My speakers also give me inspiration and motivation to continue. At these events, I present my guest speakers with the "Teabag Story Award," an acknowledgment of their courage in sharing their personal stories. When I help others to have a voice, I grow. I've done a lot of self-healing by joining support groups, making friends who support me, and giving myself reasons to move on.

Through my tea events, I also speak out and bring awareness to services that need funding. So, I'm not only helping myself but also my community. To me, the teabag is a sign of strength. The longer we steep the bag in hot water, the stronger it becomes in the end. Like me.

Through my parties, I now have a voice and am finally being heard, along with many others who participate. I also have a mental health group on Facebook called Tender Hearts, Loving Arms, as well as Miss Liz Tea Parties, and Sweet-nothing Poems, where I share links, songs, poems, and pictures of my events with the public.

By hosting tea events, I am showing my kids it is possible to move forward. I'm also showing myself.

In all my work, the steps of my growth, slowly being heard, I am becoming the person I always knew I was. I am a fighter and a survivor, I have a big heart, and I want always to be there to help others in need.

I hope my story brings you strength, hope, and courage. I know that no matter how much I've been cracked, I stand proud of who I am today. I know that I have to keep my own cup full so that I can help others. I hope this story is a cup of tea from me to you.

BIO: *Elizabeth J.O. Gagnon*

Elizabeth J.O. Gagnon (nee Hooper) is a forty-three-year-old mother of four children and three stepchildren. She has two step-grandchildren who she holds close to her heart.

One determined woman, Elizabeth has gone back to school to get her GED. She is the Founder of Miss Liz Tea Parties and Creator of The TeaBag Story Award and has been in Canada 150 stories, an online book. She writes songs and poems that she shares with churches and newspapers and in 2011, was awarded the Hope and Resilience Award from CMHA.

After completing a landscaping course, Elizabeth was featured the Cornwall Standard-Freeholder for her idea of a tea garden she hopes to have built in her community. Elizabeth feels that to have a place where people can grow mentally and emotionally also helps the community with mental illness and addiction awareness.

While Elizabeth is on disability due to mental health, she is not deterred and serves as a board member of Bereaved Families of Ontario-Cornwall, the committee for Jamming for Hospice, and volunteers in her community as much as she can. Elizabeth also loves painting, taking pictures and enjoying the solitude of nature.

Coming Out Again and Again

By Brigitte Lessard-Deyell

Some people say they always knew they were attracted to the same sex, or that they figured it out at a young age. I'm not one of them. I had practically no idea, until my first broomball tournament.

At the age of seventeen, I had been completely uprooted when my father moved our family from French-speaking Quebec to English speaking Alberta. Leaving behind my boyfriend, my friends, my culture, everything I had ever known was gone.

Now living with my parents, fresh out of high school, and looking for a new identity, I became involved in sports. I had always wanted to be on a team. Now that I was an adult, that's exactly what I was going to do. My English was limited, but I didn't need to speak English to play. Broomball was going to be my first team sport.

Not able to communicate, I became a good observer. By watching and observing facial expressions and body movement and understanding a few words here and there, I was able to follow conversations and instructions. Barely eighteen years old, I was the young one in the dressing room.

Most of the other players were in their mid to late twenties. I quickly sensed something was slightly different about a few women on the team. They were not as soft or feminine as the others. They also seemed to look at me differently.

When our first out of town tournament was announced, I was thrilled. After winning our game on the first night, it was time to celebrate. The team headed to the pub. Drinks kept landing on my table. Feeling grateful to have such good friends taking care of me, I drank them all. Little did I know that by the time I would hit the dance floor that night, my world would forever be changed.

"Dance," I shouted to the team, proud of knowing the English word.

Two of the players immediately stood up grabbed my hand, pulling me in opposite directions-they both wanted to dance with me. They seemed to be arguing about something, but I just couldn't translate. Were they arguing about dancing with me? Aren't we all dancing together? Assuming this was another cultural difference, I danced with both of them.

The next morning, I had a blurry image that kept playing over and over in my pounding head. Since I wasn't much of a drinker, the copious amount of alcohol had left my memory foggy. Did I really kiss my teammate or was it just a dream? Why couldn't I stop thinking about it? I just had to "come out" and ask her.

It turned out I didn't have to; the moment I looked at her, I knew I had kissed her. It wasn't a dream. Did the other players on the team see us?

Were they all lesbians? What did it all mean? Was I gay?

For the second time in a year, my world was turned upside-down.

The small gay community in our town in Alberta was efficient at sharing information. Within a couple of weeks, an acquaintance who often came to watch our games confronted me with the question, "Are you gay?"

"Maybe?" I didn't know the right answer. "I don't know?" To which she replied, "Can I take you out on a date?"

Confused about what closet I was in, I needed to explore, so I went on that date. It wasn't long before I knew my closet was rainbow coloured. Now that I knew what closet I was in, it was time to come out!

At that time, thirty years ago, telling someone you were gay could have huge repercussions. Many people were disowned by friends and family, lost jobs, apartments, and some even took their own lives. My first official coming out would have to be to my parents. I sat down with a piece of paper and my favorite pen to write the perfect coming out letter. What would I write? How would I write it? How would they react? Would they disown me?

I became overwhelmed with guilt. I had to make sure they knew it wasn't their fault. They had done nothing wrong. I was responsible for my "defect." I felt such guilt. How could I do this to my family? I was worried I would bring such shame. But I wrote the letter and mailed it anyway. I had no choice. This is who I was, how I felt and I was not going to live a lie. Weeks went by with no reply, nothing.

A few weeks passed, and I was missing my family. As much as I wanted to be "me," I still needed to be with my family. I was going to go for a visit and take my girlfriend with me. The long four-hour drive was nerve-wracking. Anticipating the worst, I entered the house and introduced my date. Nothing, not one negative or positive word was said. With a sigh of relief, I knew everything was going to be okay. It wasn't until years later I found out my mother cried when she read the letter, but then reasoned with herself that I was still the same person I always had been. For that understanding, I was truly grateful.

Coming out to friends and family can be very painful. Once the words are said, there is no going back. Just like a tattoo, once the ink has dried, you can't make it disappear. Sure you can change your mind and have the ink lazered off, but it never can be completely erased.

My next big coming out story was bizarre. Now in my early twenties, I had been in a relationship for two years with a woman twelve years my senior. She was an extremely possessive, closeted police officer. She had my whole life planned, including our retirement.

The once comforting feeling of being taken care of was long gone, and I was suffocating. I knew leaving her wasn't going to be easy. But once again, I needed to be true to myself. On one of her days off, I told her I was leaving her and then left the house. She drove to her precinct, loaded an unmarked police car with a shotgun, a handgun, bullets, and beer. She then drove to the house where I was and dropped off a box with my name on it. When I opened the box, it was filled with items from our house that would prove she was gay. She then drove west into the mountains and shot herself.

When I received the call from her Sergeant, all I was told was the hospital she was at and that she was alive for now. No one offered to drive me safely to the hospital, as they would have done for a spouse. He then called her parents. At thirty-two years of age, her next of kin was her parents, certainly not her "roommate."

Media was all over the story. The newspaper headline read: "Police officer shoots herself after being jilted by her lover." On the 5 o'clock news, out of focus, voice disguised, the sister of a friend who didn't even know us, was explaining to the world what had happened. The media was hungry for a story, and we were in hiding. She was in the hospital under a pseudo name and I, at my friend's house.

Later that night, I received a call from her parents. Of course, they wanted to know what was going on. They'd be on the next flight. I picked them up at the airport and took them to a hotel, explaining they would be hounded by the media at our house and had to stay somewhere else.

I sat them down, and gently opened the closet doors of their thirty-two-year-old daughter. I also had to explain that I was the cause of her suicide attempt. I don't remember much from that conversation. I was on some kind of autopilot.

Too young to know better, I agreed to stay in the house of my now ex-girlfriend, to help her get back on her feet. But I made it clear it was over. A year later, still living with her, I met someone new. She was beautiful, feminine, and soft and had a boyfriend. And to my amazement the attraction was mutual. I moved out to my parent's basement suite so that I could rebuild my life. When I realized I was in love, I knew I had to be with her. I also knew this coming out was going to bring even more drama to my life. She was from a small town and an extremely religious family.

The first person she would come out to was her sister with whom she had just purchased a house. Immediately the deal had to be killed, and she was bought out of the mortgage. Next, it would be coming out to her parents. Their response was biblical: "The devil winked at you, and you smiled back." She was devastated.

The church sent ministers over, trying to pull her out of this homosexual hell. They tried to segregate her from me so they could reason with her, but she would have none of it. If I were not included, she would have no part of it. We were in love, and nothing would change that. She didn't see or speak to her parents, or most of her family, for over two years. Slowly things got better, and one by one, they became more comfortable with our relationship.

After ten happy years together, my biological clock got so loud it vibrated my whole body. Now thirty-five, I wanted children. In the 90's it was still extremely uncommon for lesbians to be mothers, but I knew of one couple who had done it. But my partner did not want children. I was devastated.

For some reason, I had assumed she would love to have a family. I mourned for a few months but eventually came to accept my fate. I was not going to be a mother. But I did have a great life with plenty of money, traveling the world, great friends; I would be ok.

That's when my future wife entered my life. And even though we were both in a relationship and I was a faithful, committed partner, my attraction to her was intense. We became fast friends. She was beautiful, funny and smart. We got closer and closer. We started talking about children. She confided in me that she was convinced she was going to have children one day, just not with the partner she was with. That rocked my world. I was in love with her.

I stood there at a fork on my road to happiness. One road I knew so well; it was a road I had been on for ten years. It was safe and enjoyable, with a clear destination on the map. The other road I knew nothing about. But on that road was my most prized treasure in life: motherhood. I made one of the most difficult decisions of my life and left her.

Since she hadn't told her family she was gay, once again, we would have to come out of the closet. This time it would be easy and funny...for me anyway. My soon-to-be wife was terrified of rejection, just like I had been twenty years earlier. Her coming out party happened over the phone. During a conversation with her sister, the topic came up. A friend's daughter had just come out of the closet. That's when her sister asked, "So when are you going to come out?"

To which my love replied jokingly, "How about right now?!" "Perfect," said her sister, and said she had to hang up and call everyone. It turns out it was the worst kept secret in the family!

After seventeen years together, married with two kids, we're still coming out of the closet, over and over again. Every time we introduce each other to someone new, it's always a mini coming out of the closet event. The fact that we both look feminine and are married with two children makes people assume we have husbands.

Having the same last name often makes people ask if we are related. It always amuses me to watch their reactions when I reply, "Yes, she's my wife."

It has been interesting seeing the reaction change over the past thirty years. I had people argue with me that I wasn't gay because I looked too much like a woman. One person was shocked when she found out I was gay because I was "so nice." These days the reaction is to "stay cool" as people try not to react, though you can almost hear the wheels turning. My favourite coming out was when my wife was pregnant, and people would ask us, "how did that happen?" to which we would reply, "We don't know. It was an accident"!

Coming out, again and again, has taught me the importance of being true to yourself and standing up for your truth, no matter the cost. Coming out has thought me to be brave and bold. It has made me the fearless leader I am, one that empowers women to rise up and proudly stand in their truth.

BIO: *Brigitte Lessard-Deyell*

Wife, mother of two, entrepreneur, author, and visionary, Brigitte has spent most of her life supporting and empowering women through numerous female-based businesses. Whether it's at the microphone or on camera, you will instantly be moved by Brigitte's larger than life energy.

Passionate about women having the opportunity to share their stories in a positive and uplifting environment, Brigitte created Women Talk; a monthly event which has already spread to many cities across the country including an annual convention; "The Wonder of You." Her gift of Cultural Integration brings together women from all social classes, religion, sexual orientation, and race and encourages them to respect and celebrate their differences.

Brigitte is a Certified Sacred Gifts Guide and has studied and practices the Law of Attraction's principals for almost 20 years. As a motivational speaker, Brigitte inspires women to celebrate their feminine energy, to speak their truth and stand fully in their power.
www.womentalk.ca www.sportsbras.ca
https://www.facebook.com/BrigitteKLessardDeyell
https://www.linkedin.com/ in/brigittelessard-deyell/

The Journey Home

By Colleen Herbst

*O*n a cold stormy winter day in February 2011, a gust of wind shook the house in Lethbridge as the phone rang. It was a lawyer from Montana that I knew.

When I got off the phone, I immediately called my husband, Calvin. By the time I hung up from talking to him, I knew my life was changed forever.

In 1980, I met Calvin in university, and a few years later after we got married, we were living and working in Los Angles. Every day when I drove to work I saw the Hollywood sign; I had to pinch myself because I was truly living the life of my dreams in one of the most exciting cities in the world.

At thirty years of age, I was pregnant with our first child. The day before my due date, on August 21, 1988, it was a hot, beautiful Sunday afternoon. To take my mind off things, Calvin and I hopped into my two-seater, black sports car and headed to Malibu. Suddenly, out of the corner of my eye, I saw a big black American car coming right at us. Later I learned it was traveling at 90 mph.

The next thing I remembered was the ambulance driver saying, "Mother dead. Try to save the baby."

I was scared.

They rushed me into UCLA medical center, and without any warning or drugs, they cut into me and ripped my baby out of me. During the second surgery, I saw the paddles coming down on top of me and thought, why does everyone think I'm dead? I'm not dead.

After the third surgery, I woke up in a coma. And I was pissed! I wanted to live, and I decided I was going to be the best at recovery anyone had ever seen.

I started visualizing my toes moving, then my feet, next my legs, sitting, standing and finally walking. My body was badly broken. My brain could not remember how to read, write, walk or talk. My road back was not quick or easy. All I had was faith and hope. These were my only tools in my toolbox.

It took me five years to learn how to read at a fifth-grade level, another ten years to get to a high school level. Fifteen years to read music and play the piano again. I did learn to walk and then run again which is something I always loved to do. Running down the roads, up the hills, and now the stairs saying, "My body is strong, I can run, I can talk, I can read."

This, along with the rhythm and cadence of my feet reprogrammed my body and brain and got me functioning again. I also discovered I had this gift of fortitude, the inner thing that helped me drag myself out of bed every day and fight through the pain to recapture my life.

My baby Haley survived the accident, but her injuries were severe.

A few years later, her pediatrician in Santa Monica found an innovative brain injury institute in Philadelphia where they trained me to be the therapist, teacher, cheerleader, and leader of the road to recovery. This meant a rigorous schedule, but I felt like I had to do everything possible to try to keep Haley alive. Even though she was so brain injured she could barely inhale or exhale, I believed in possibilities. For ten years I worked twelve hours a day following a brain injury recovery program. Haley got a little bit better. I got a lot better.

In 1996, in a most delightful twist, I adopted two more girls, Shea and Quinn. I felt blessed! We left Los Angeles to move to Whitefish, Montana. Our lives were busy, fun, and challenging because I was raising three daughters, and still working on our recovery. I was mostly parenting alone because after Calvin's business failed in Montana, he got jobs in Chicago and Santa Barbara and only came home once a month.

By this time, I had noticed extreme mood swings. I didn't know exactly what to do, or who to talk to. I decided to make the best of it. When Calvin was fired from both jobs, he came back to Whitefish and found part-time work. But things got worse in 2008 when the US recession hit. Work was hard to find. We all moved to Lethbridge, Alberta, Canada. We rented a tiny house, moved a few things and Calvin found a job. We kept our house in Whitefish for weekend vacationing because Lethbridge and Whitefish were only 3 hours apart and I hoped we would return to Whitefish, the place I loved the most.

That brings me back to that life-changing snowy day in Lethbridge in 2011, when the phone rang. I remember that ringtone so well, that when I hear that ringtone on other people's cell phones, it makes me sick to my stomach. On the other end of the phone was a lawyer from Whitefish. I listened to what she said in complete silence. I could barely respond. I think I said something like, "I'll get back to you," but I really don't remember. All I remember is that my life changed in an instant.

I hung up the phone and knew my whole life had been a lie. I remember asking myself, "How could I have been so stupid?" The lawyer told me that Calvin hadn't paid any bills, income tax, or property tax for ten years.

The lawyer said that the Sheriff was delivering notices that our properties were being seized.

At that point, I went numb.

When I phoned Calvin to tell him, he said nothing!

That night we drove to Whitefish in silence, through a snowstorm to move all our belongings out of our Whitefish house and into a local storage facility. My Whitefish friends were there to help, and we had to go quickly go through every room to decide what got stored and what got trashed. I remember so clearly my friend taking me out to my husband's office in the back of the garage to show me what he found. I nearly threw up.

Ten years of my life was hiding in the unopened mail that Calvin had tucked away in nooks, crannies, boxes, and bags. The shock of seeing all of this slapped me into the reality of the seriousness of Calvin's dysfunction and deceit. All I was thinking was what next?

Well, the next thing I found out was that he was doing the same thing in Canada too. I went on the hunt looking through everything and found more bad behavior and lies. Drugs, alcohol, porn, smoking, the list seemed endless. The problems were overwhelming. I did not have the skills or knowledge to fix this. I was beaten down.

In two months, I swelled five dress sizes. My cortisol production was off the charts. Adrenalin pumped through my body non-stop. I had nightmares. I didn't sleep for years. I ground down my teeth. I was fat, angry, depressed, afraid, unhappy, disappointed, hopeless, and couldn't stop crying. I was a mess, and I looked it. I was worried the stress was going to kill me. My friends thought I was going to have a stroke at any moment. I isolated from everyone except my brothers and sisters and my children.

Four years later, on July 30, 2014, Calvin blurted out that he wished I had died in the car accident.

In a moment of clarity, I understood why he destroyed our marriage and family's financial security. He hated his life, responsibilities, job, marriage, limitations, himself, and me. He was trying to get me to leave, but I didn't get the memo. I am not a quitter, and that damn near killed me.

Immediately this clarity lifted my spirit and released the physical pain from my body. I felt free of constraints that I didn't even know were weighing me down. I heard, "You need to go, you are meant to be happy and have love."

I knew that I was done. Within a few days, I packed up the kids and left.

I discovered that the ex, the tax department, and the financial advisors didn't care if this problem ever got solved. It had all turned into a game of power, and manipulation between all the players. No one cared about me, my kids, or the injustice of it all. This was taking a huge emotional toll on me. My brothers, sisters, and a few key friends stepped in and pulled me up out of the abyss of depression. They strapped me into a suit of armour, and gave me the words and courage to stand up for myself against these men and the system. Then shit got done.

I dug deep into the same mental fortitude I had lying on that operating table all those years ago. I got angry, and I went to battle to save my life and the future of myself and kids. It was time to focus on my future and believe that I could get through this. I used every mindset technique, vision board, mantra, affirmations, and discipline I had used to recover from the accident. This had worked for me before, and I knew it would work again.

First, I created my divorce plan and strategy. Then I started to build my team. I hired a divorce attorney who worked with me to help with the legal side, while I negotiated the terms of the divorce and settlement with Calvin. This helped me save a lot of money.

Next, I put together expert coaches from other disciplines because there were no Certified Divorce Coaches available back then. I assigned everyone, including friends and family, a job description of how they could support me emotionally while keeping me present and accountable on the business side of the divorce process.

It helped me get organized, and prioritize the financial paperwork, deal with the ex, communicate with the lawyer, and address all the issues that were going to affect my children. I created a daily planner that I called the "Get Shit Done Planner," which helped me accomplish actionable steps each day in the business side of the divorce, while simultaneously helping me through the emotional healing and recovery.

My planner reminded me to do my affirmations, visualizations, exercise, nutrition, and stress releasing activities each day. I set 90-day transformation goals, and the planner kept me on track. I was re- inventing myself, changing my mindset, building my confidence and self- esteem, all the while knocking off tasks on my divorce list. With each completed task and decision, I became more empowered. This planner saved me time, money, grief, heartache and stress.

I went to counselling, therapy, and group support of all kinds. I was determined to find my voice and my true self. I knew that if I could do that, I could get to the other side of this shit storm and find the life I was always meant to have.

I built a vision board of how I wanted my life to be, what mattered, how it would make me feel and who I would be. I created a happy list – things that would make me happy. All of this gave me balance so that my daily life was more than the long to do lists of very important business and divorce matters.

By summer of 2015, my future seemed brighter and attainable. I achieved everything on my vision board and happy list, so I created another one. My transformation happened.

July 6, 2017, I watched my three daughters, and six more children walk down a path in a mountain meadow towards wedding arches by the Flathead River, near Whitefish Montana. Tears were flowing down my cheeks. I was so happy. I could see in my mind everything I had been through the past 29 years.

Faith, hope, fortitude, positivity, and courage stood by me all the way through my life. They helped me overcome my injuries, raise kind happy children, recover from my divorce and build up my coaching practice. After I wrote, "Breathe, How I Trained Myself Back to Life," I traveled North America speaking about my journey.

That was when I discovered that I didn't want to be known for only being resilient or inspirational. I wanted to be known for being happy. I wanted others to know that they can be happy no matter what they have been through. And I wanted one more thing.

As the last child took their place beside the arches, Arlyn gently took my arm and steadied me as we began to walk towards our nine children and the wedding arches. I could hear the beautiful lyrics of Christina Perri's "A Thousand Years," floating over the mountain meadow.

I have died every day waiting for you darling, Don't be afraid. I have loved you for a thousand years I'll love you for a thousand more.

The tears of joy turned into a big grin when I saw all our smiling families and friends who had gathered to celebrate our wonderful, glorious wedding day with us.

This was the day when my whole life finally made sense to me. I was grateful for my life, my three beautiful kind children, that phone call, the long winding journey back to my hometown, and the wisdom and grace to recognize and accept Arlyn's love when he walked into my life.

It was love that I wanted.

Bio: *Colleen Herbst*

Colleen grew up on a farm in Alberta, Canada. The youngest of eight children, she was encouraged by her parents to have a big plan for life. After graduating from the University of Alberta, she went off to Los Angles to pursue her dreams. Then life took a few twists and turns, and it brought Colleen right back home to the start. Just down the road from where she grew up, was a boy she never met, who'd stayed firmly planted where he grew up.

By happenstance, they met all these many years later. Arlyn, who had been a widow for eight years, felt like he was waiting for Colleen to come home. They are now married. Arlyn is the love of Colleen's life, and together they have nine children. Shea and Quinn are currently in university pursuing their dreams. Haley lives at a nearby care center where she goes to day programs and activities. Haley is happy, and Colleen feels a sense of peace. All nine children are happy and grateful that their parents found love.

Colleen (Hierath) Herbst is the author of "Breath, How I trained Myself Back to Life," "Frock Off" (anthology edition), "Sacred Hearts Rising Anthology: Breaking the Silence One Story at a Time. Book 1, Chapter title: The Journey Home," and "Exhale" (2019)

Divorce Recovery Coaching: Colleen combined twenty-five years of human resources, recruiting and consulting experience with Certified Divorce Coaching so she can provide others with the kind of expertise she needed when she was divorcing. She helps women navigate the emotional roller coaster, while simultaneously managing the business of divorce. Her mission is to help people regain their focus, get happy again, set new life and career goals, and design the life they want for their second act.

Coaching Services Include: 90 Day Transformation, 3 Stages of Break-Up Recovery, Divorce Resolution Process and Break-Up Recovery Retreats

Email Colleen to schedule a complimentary discovery call so that she can see how she can best serve your needs and receive a copy of Top 10 Divorce Mistakes to Avoid.

www.TheDivorceRecovery.com
DivorceCoach@TheDivorceRecovery.com

You Are Enough

By Michele Noordhof

*I*n August of last year, at the end of the workday, I was traveling the secondary highway west towards the mountains, mesmerized by their beauty and majesty. A reflection of light caught my eye, and I looked into the other lane. As the vehicle passed me, I was momentarily frozen in space and time. I realized that my usual desire to jump into the oncoming lane was no longer there. Instead, a deep peace, a holy presence, softly enveloped me in self-love. This was so very new to me, and I basked in the warmth of it.

A few months earlier, I'd come to understand that I could no longer sustain the life path I was on. Simple, yet profound words, from my friend, "You are enough." The quiet whisper, asking me to listen, to accept these words and the truth they spoke. It was time to find my way, the life path meant for me.

I realized that to move forward, that I would first have to go back. I wasn't sure if I could go back or if I wanted to, but I knew that I needed to revisit those memories and experiences that I had worked so hard to ignore and forget. I also knew that I could no longer pretend that my past, and the beliefs that I carried within myself, as a result, had never existed. So

121

taking a step back in time I began the journey of my self- discovery and remembrance.

My first childhood home was an old two-story house that sat on top of a hill surrounded by farmland. I can still see it in my mind's eye, dark and looming against the landscape, a sentinel, guarding the secrets there. I have some fond memories of that time, but it's the other memories that I think of; some so clear it seems like they happened just yesterday and others almost out of reach for me.

As they came back to me, I began to learn that these memories had created the story that I believed about me -that the world did not need or want me, and in fact, the world would be a better place without me.

I remembered a family event when I was sitting in my high chair, and I threw up and was spanked for what I did. Another memory was of me lying in the crib on my back, my pajamas and the blanket covering me being attached to the mattress with safety pins so I could not roll over then left in the dark, alone. Then the time I was scrubbed so hard with a bar of soap I was raw everywhere, being told that I deserved it; I was a dirty girl.

From the period between ages four and five, I don't have a lot of memories. I do remember always being frightened of the upstairs part of the house, terrified that something evil was coming to get me. Sometimes I would hear the whistle of the trains that would travel along the rail line just a few miles east of where we were, and I would run to hide. Around that time I started having a recurring nightmare that stayed with me until well into my thirties.

When I was six, one of my regular chores was to wash the floors. I would have a dishpan filled with soapy water, and off I would go to wash them. This particular day I miss-stepped and splashed water on the floor. My mother was instantly angry. She grabbed me by the arms, yelling "What's wrong with you? You could do a better job when you were four. You always do everything wrong. You will never be able to do anything right."

I quietly cried as I died inside that day. I would be haunted by this memory throughout my life, living the belief formed in this defining moment.

When I was seven my parents bought an old small house closer to town, it was just off the side of the highway. I was happy to move away from the other house and all the things that frightened me there. Shortly after we moved there, my mother asked me to sit on the living room floor where she said that she was not my mother.

I sat shocked as the many questions came forth about where my mother was, why she had left me and if she was coming for me. I didn't understand who this person was in front of me who I had been calling Mother. There were no answers from her except to tell me that I had not been wanted and was left behind at the hospital. I learned too that day that my parents had lost a child, Rosie and since they could not have any more children they adopted me. That was the end of the talk; my mother never even told me that she loved me.

Shortly after that, I started going to Sunday school with my aunt. I looked forward to attending each week. I absorbed each new thing I learned, eager to use it in my life. My newly found faith was quickly tested; however when I was told that I had better pray that my dad would come home. He had disappeared for a few days, and my mom did not know where he was. Each night that he didn't return, she told me that I was not praying hard enough. He did eventually return home having been on a bender with some buddies for a few days. Though my prayers were answered, it seemed that I had not done enough.

At the beginning of junior high, some of the boys on the school bus tormented me, relentlessly. They would take the rotting garbage and smear it over my face and through my hair, calling me horrible names. I was too small to fight them off, and the bus driver never seemed to notice or didn't care. When I finally dared to talk to my mother, she told me that she could not help me. The mothers of these kids were her friends from her community ladies group, and she did not want to upset them. I was devastated; there was no one to help me.

At twelve, I attempted suicide for the first time. It was a poor attempt but the emotions I felt and the story about who I thought I was, were very real. I kept the suicide attempt a secret; I was too terrified to find out what might happen to me if my mother found out.

At seventeen I tried to run away, but I was too afraid. Still, I knew I couldn't stay. This was my next attempt to commit suicide. It was not a success either, and I fled as soon as I was eighteen, marrying my first boyfriend. Two years into the marriage he committed a violent crime, sending him to prison and leaving me homeless.

This dark time in my life led to another suicide attempt. With help from some friends I survived this attempt and tried to pick up the pieces to move on.
I did not have a good sense of my value and worth, and I continued to make poor choices that created a spiral of emotional turmoil. Two relationships later I was trying to make a go of things. We had two beautiful children, and I had returned to my Christian faith, but I was still haunted. Every time something went wrong I immediately went back to my old belief that the world would be better without me.

I even went back to that house on the hill to try to face the demons. I walked from room to room and tried to capture the whispers from within. I only felt sadness and loss. As I left that house, I looked into my rearview mirror to see my four-year-old self, crying and banging on the top floor window, trapped in that horrible little house. I sobbed uncontrollably that day as I drove away. I did not how to rescue her.

A time came where I thought I could finally find the peace I needed from all the hurts and wounds. I had a suicide plan and was ready to execute it, but two of my colleagues who recognized the signs staged an intervention. I agreed to live, but I died a worse death waiting for each day to pass, counting it as one day less I would have to live. I created a façade of living, while the rest of world around me had no idea of my inner turmoil.

In November 2013 I attended a gala; it was a film release for a documentary called "The Jen Unplugged Uplife Project." Jen's story and her message about living life fiercely and out loud spoke deeply to me. I had recently met Jen through a dear friend, Sylvie. Both of these remarkable women were fighting hard to live and to love life each day, showing gratitude for every moment. I found myself asking what had happened to me, why did I not see life this way. I could not continue to live in this valley of death pretending to be alive nor could I end it all; being selfish by throwing my life away.

Slowly I began to seek ways that I could move away from the valley I had been hiding in. I chose to focus on positive thoughts and to find gratitude. It did make a difference on the surface. It helped to keep the dark thoughts at bay, but it wasn't all that I needed. "You are enough," my friend had said to me. There was a gentle whisper that stirred within me. This would be an important moment, one that would lead me to an open door that would change my life.

A few weeks later I saw a coupon for a ninety-minute float therapy session. That same gentle whisper was telling me that I needed to go. I didn't want to go alone so I called my girlfriend and she came with me, offering encouragement and support.

The room was pitch black except for a tear-shaped pod in the one corner. As I prepared to enter the pod, I allowed myself just to be. I stepped into the thick salty water and floated on my back, listening to the soft music under the glow of the purplish colored light. For the first sixty minutes my mind was filled with chattering monkeys, but during the last thirty minutes, I experienced release and rest I'd never known. As I let the water hold me up, I felt the holy presence softly speaking to me with words of love and affirmation. Again I heard those words, "you are enough." Then I saw a door; it was being held open for me. I stepped through. This would be the beginning of my self-discovery and remembrance.

Over the weeks that followed my float therapy experience, I began to learn about myself, recalling the memories of my childhood and the impact they had. Then other memories began also to come back, but these were different. They were of moments in my life when I had allowed myself to open up, trusting in the holy presence around me. It was during one of these moments of remembering when she emerged from the darkness, a tall warrior with a shield and a spear. She rose up behind me, dressed in full armor and I knew that she was the remembrance of who I was and that she would stand in the gap to battle for my life.

I found strength, power, and protection at that moment. I knew that I was no longer a victim of my circumstances and no longer losing the battle for my life. I saw my life as something so much more; it had purpose and meaning. A reason to live, not die. With my warrior woman standing with me, I stepped forward into my new life, fully armed with a vision to create a new path, a new direction and a life that I would never have thought possible.

Many of us have memories that have defined us and tied us to a place and time that seeks to destroy us. The more we ignore it and bury it, the more we become attached to the words we associate with those moments, the story that becomes us.

My old story had convinced me that the world did not want me or need me; that in fact, the world would be a better place without me. This created a belief system that I was not good enough, that I would never do anything right, and that I was unwanted and unloved. I also believed that I was unimportant, unworthy and a disappointment to those around me. My mantra became "death is better than life." Somehow though, I could not even get dying right which just added to the failure I thought I was.

Looking back, I can see that I wore a mask, being an actor in a play who hid her pain that she felt inside while she struggled between life and death. But there was a world that existed outside of the story I had written for myself and that world fought hard for me to see my authentic truth. Then that one day I finally found the right door, opening it wide.

I learned that I needed to choose to listen to the message from within and not to seek validation from the world around me, especially from those I felt had authority over me. This was the first step to discovering self-love and rewriting my story and the beliefs I had about myself. To accept that I am amazing, beautiful, worthy of love and acceptance. That I am important, valued, loved and good enough.

Some days, I slip back into the old beliefs, but I try to no longer stay in that place, fighting my way back to where I am meant to be. I am learning how to hold my little four-year-old self and to fill her up with love so she too can release the past and know her story—the real story of who she is. Together we rise from the ashes, find healing and live each day with gratitude that we are here.

BIO: *Michele Noordhof*

At age twelve, Michele attempted suicide. This would not be the only time in her life that she would walk this close to death. The story that had been written in her life told her that ending her life would be the best thing she could do, this world did not need her or want her and, in fact, the world would be better without her.

In 2016 Michele experienced an awakening deeper than anything she had ever encountered. She saw how her old story had been a lie to distract her from discovering her true self and the message she is called to share. Michele has embarked on a new path to rewrite her story, not only to change her life but also to help others break the lies of their old stories and to find freedom in who they are meant to be in this world.

To learn more about her journey, please check out
www.thewellspringofhope.com

The Present I Choose

By Bonnie Todd

I am not defined by what has happened to me in the past, but by what I have chosen to do about it in the present. Numbing the pain with alcohol and drugs was becoming unbearable and changes needed to happen. Given that my past is full of so much pain making strong life changing choices in the present has not been easy. It is these hard decisions in life that define us.

My mother was a gold digger, and when my Dad caught her cheating, he left without a thought. She soon married the man she was caught with, and he became my step-dad. We became a part of the Johnstone family, a wealthy family in small-town Fort Langley. We lived on the 50-acre family property and had all the luxuries money can buy. Looking back it is like we were in a soap opera with all the drama that ensued; money, addiction, and scandal.

My new grandmother was in the spotlight because of her career, and she was also a very well-known public figure in the business world. My mother, a product of the intergenerational trauma of the sixties, where the taking of aboriginal children from their families to be placed in foster homes was common. She suffered from many addictions. My step-dad took on the role of being a father to me but had suffered his own traumas that are unknown, as my grandma adopted all of her children. The cycle of abuse and trauma continued with me.

I cannot remember when it started, but my earliest recollection of my stepdad is him standing over my bed and telling me I was his special girl, and that this special time together was our secret. He had molested me for years. When I was nine, I walked into my mother watching Oprah. The topic was sexual abuse, and I found myself intrigued, asking her what sexual abuse was. My mom is a survivor of abuse, and she explained to me the best she could, and I instantly had a name for what Charlie was doing to me. I ran to my room and started writing in my diary that I was sexually abused. My diary was filled with pain and included all my secrets, and how I felt towards my parents. My mom was mean, physically abusive, and somewhat vengeful towards me. Page after page, my diary expressed rage towards them both and how much I hated them.

The day the secret came out I was about nine years old, in grade four, and my mom was picking me up early from school. The panic starts to set in; the thoughts are racing through my head.

What have I done? Will she beat me?

She shows me my diary. My throat drops into the deep pit of my stomach, and I shrink down to the smallest I've ever been in my entire life. I wasn't worried about her knowing my secret, but that she is going to beat me for all the horrible things I wrote about her in that diary. At nine, I had full recognition of swear words, and how to use them. I'd been hanging around my aunt since I was five, and she is ten years older than me, so to understand and fully imagine, it's as if I skipped childhood completely. I was always a pretty grown-up kid. What happened next is a blur, but there was a separation, moving around, foster care, counseling, and a nose dive into the abyss of severe drug use by both my parents.

All I wanted was a family that was proud of me, to be famous, and for everyone to like me. Living with my mom drained me of all life I had in me. She made me feel so insignificant and worthless I moved out around the age of 13, to Charlie's house. This is probably why many people thought I made up the molestation allegations, but no one knew how horrible it was living with my mom.

At least at Charlie's, I got to see my grandma more, and be spoiled and given whatever I wanted. At least at Charlie's, I got the clothes I wanted for school and wasn't teased for how I dressed, or for crying all the time because my mom had me feeling like I was a waste of skin. When she said, "I brought you into this world; I can take you out," I feared the day she would "take me out." My mom never understood why I would have this man in my life, so she believed I was having sexual relations with him and would tell people this. I never knew this until I was 36, but it now made sense to me why I was accused of liking to "fuck" my dad by a very abusive ex-boyfriend when we were together.

By 14, I dropped out of school, and drinking and boys became my number one priority. I was wild, to say the least, popping pills and trying to get high with psychedelics by 15, and traveling with the carnival just to get away. At this point, Charlie was using needles, and his addiction was growing out of control. By 16, I was running away to California for a man in his twenties, hoping he would save me. I never did find what I was looking for, and to be honest I am not sure what exactly it was I yearned for. Stability and normalcy is my guess. So, you get the idea I ran from my feelings and my problems and covered up my past with alcohol and men. I thought at 21 I had my life figured out. I was in love with a man 14 years older than me and had two babies a year apart from each other. Boy, was I wrong! I had no idea how hard life could be.

By 24, I was a single mom, my grandma passed away, my family no longer felt like family, and I felt an obligation to take care of Charlie, so he lived in my basement. Past trauma would not let me move on in life, but instead of dealing with it, I turned to alcohol and copious amounts of cocaine. Of course, to everyone looking in, I was just another Indian addicted to booze, and drugs. I cried out for help; I voiced how Charlie needed to get his own house, and for me to sell my house and move on. This did not happen and instead my house, that was in trust for me, was sold and I had to figure life out.

So I latched on to my abusive boyfriend at the time and moved in with him on the reserve. Due to our lifestyle and my boyfriend's criminal history, I lost custody of my children. I dreamed of leaving this unhealthy relationship but did not know how to leave him and "figure" life out. I regained custody back after giving birth to my third child. I went from no kids on May 2nd, to one newborn on the 3rd, to three kids on the 5th. Although the abuse had dwindled, so had my love for this man. I left him finally after planning it for years.

In 2015, I married my current husband, and after more than a year together, it was past due for us to grow up, and finally show up in life. His brother passed away from an overdose, and it hit us hard. We all used drugs together frequently, and his brother was living with us a week before his death. I haven't touched cocaine or alcohol since October 16, 2016, and my husband has maintained his sobriety as well. Together, we fight addiction and ending the cycle, so my kids don't continue the cycle.

Then I lost my handicapped brother, and all the emotions came rushing in. I cried for him, but feeling this pain sober brought up all the trauma I had never fully grieved from. Feeling true emotion for the first time is damn hard, but worth more than all the money in the world. Being able to feel pain, talk through the pain, and move past the pain has given me a new lease on life.

A few key moments that have changed my life forever is taking control of my mind, and is the single most important thing I have done. Without being sober, I am not able to move past the trauma, and I used to numb myself to it by getting loaded which NEVER solved anything. Also, I stood up to my parents because of my values. I finally put myself and my feelings first. No longer do I worry how my actions are affecting them. The two people who had a duty to protect me from harm no longer can harm me. They failed me completely, and I let them know that. I wrote them a letter that said, "I remember! You failed me! Please let me go!"

Sending them that letter made me feel free, weightless, and no longer ashamed of something I had no right to be ashamed of.

Speaking out about the abuse and choosing to share my story with the world is the most courageous thing I have done. By sharing my story, my hope is other survivors will have the courage to stand up and begin the healing. Every day I do my gratitude check-in and just enjoy where I am at that moment. L ife is a precious gift, and I am grateful to be here, alive and sober and enjoying it.

It is my time to come first. The cycle ends with me.

BIO: *Bonnie Todd*

Bonnie Todd is a public speaker fighting the war on shame. Knowing that shame keeps her sick, she chooses to fight it head on so she can have a life worth living. An aspiring writer, Bonnie's next plan is to write her memoir. She refers to herself as a badass in everything she does.

Once gripped by anxiety and the fear of others opinions, she now lives a pretty normal life in Abbotsford, BC with her husband Kyle, and three children Jack, Lucille, and William, dog Bella, and cats Askem and Whiskers.

Bonnie has just begun living her life with meaning, and her mission is to empower women everywhere to do the same.

On the Wings of an Angel

By Tannis Soderquist

*T*his October 11 will mark the 16th birthday of my first daughter, Jaidin, who sadly passed away when she was seven days old from a rare kidney disease.

Having my first child pass away at such a young age, and being helpless to help her was something that I had, never in my wildest dreams, ever thought would be what my life would hold.

The past 16 years have had some very hard times in dealing with Jaidin's death. You are never fully prepared as a pregnant woman, to have to go through a pregnancy, all the hopes and dreams, thinking of the future and planning, only to have them stomped out completely like the last glowing ember of a fire slowly dying down.

When we first found out that anything was wrong with our daughter, I was in the middle of labor, the nurse had checked to see how dilated I was and she thought that the baby was breech. They whisked me to the ultrasound tech, and that is when they discovered that Jaidin's kidneys were 4x the normal size, and completely full of masses.

135

From there was a whirlwind of emotions, I was scared, not sure what was going on, in extreme pain, and trying to be positive that everything would be ok, and we would deal with a sick baby, never thinking that she would pass away.

My doctor had the Neonatal team fly to us into Peace River, (he was sure I would deliver on the plane, and with a breech baby with problems, the risk of losing both of us was high). Once they landed, the surgical team prepped me for surgery, and before I knew it, I was numb from the chest down.

Within minutes the Caesarian had been started and then Jaidin was born. They gave me a quick glimpse of her as the Neo-Natal team took over and intubated her and prepped her for the flight from Peace River to Edmonton.

I heard the news that night from the Doctor at the NICU, that she had a 1% chance of survival, so now began the hard and heartbreaking task of preparing myself to lose my child, but still maintain some semblance of hope that maybe a miracle would occur, and she would somehow survive, because God really couldn't be that cruel, could he?

We spent seven days at the University of Alberta's Neo-Natal Intensive Care Unit or NICU, learning all about this disease that Jaidin had been born with.

Autosomal Recessive Polycystic Kidney Disease, the name was longer than my daughter. We found out that my ex-husband and I are both carriers and have a chance of having more children born with the disease. We learned that Jaidin, liked to be sung to, and she loved her little brown stuffed doggy. She loved to be held, especially when her heart rate got dangerously high and the nurses would worry. I spent many a late night, in the quiet of the hospital, with just the beeps and blips of the monitors, holding my tiny daughter and praying for a miracle. That was when I started to lose my faith in God, and that he can't save innocent children.

Jaidin passed away in my arms on her 7th day of her short life that was filled with so much love. It was almost surreal after the nurse swaddled my dead daughter, and carried her like she was still living. In those moments, I didn't feel like myself. I felt like this terrible tragedy had not happened to me. It felt like a bad nightmare was finally over.

I don't think I really cried, like sobbing hard, gut-wrenching cries until we got back to my mom's place that night she passed away. Getting ready to take a shower and looking in the mirror at my scar, the stretch marks and the breasts full of useless milk, hit me like a ton of bricks. I had nothing to show for my pain, my heartache except that I had lost a child. No baby to take home and watch grow.

I broke down and cried in the shower, milk running everywhere, I just didn't care anymore. What could I do? I had no training for this, no preparation in how to deal with this. None of us did.

Not only had we lost a daughter, but grandparents lost a grandchild, and two aunts had lost a niece.

I honestly don't remember anything more of the weeks after we lost Jaidin, I was in a depression. People didn't know what to say to me; I didn't know how to respond, or react when they expressed their sorrow. I just wanted people to leave me alone and let me live in solitude and anger.

I hated God, cursed his name for taking my child while perverts and pedophiles and murderers and rapists were still drawing breath. It made me angry to think the God had no compassion, he just let her die, and I couldn't do a damn thing to stop it. Over the years this anger has gone away and replaced by indifference to Gods miracles and the belief that if one has faith things will be ok.

I do remember sitting at the kitchen table and thinking to myself "I have two choices, I can start to drink to take the pain away, or I can start to live again and let each day get better and better."

I chose the latter because the first option held no appeal to me.

I had gotten a kitten when I was pregnant, and Otis became my baby, he was there for me when we lost Jaidin. In his cat way, he knew that I needed comfort and loving, between him and my other kitten Dewey; they helped me to start to heal and get the emotional support I was not getting from my ex-husband, who simply just pushed his pain down and didn't deal with it. I sometimes think that he blamed me for what happened.

Each day, month and year got better, easier to breathe and live, I could find happiness again. Then I got pregnant for the second time. Luckily there is a test that can be performed early on in the pregnancy that can determine if the new baby would be born with the same disease or not. So, I was to drive to Edmonton to the Royal Alex Hospital and undergo a CVS or Chorionic Vilnius Sampling. They injected a big needle into me and the placenta, and took an actual piece of the new baby's DNA and tested it against Jaidin's, to see if the specific gene anomaly was present. The test took three weeks to come back.

3 WEEKS!!!!!

That was a hellish wait, not knowing if I was going to carry a healthy baby to term or have to abort the pregnancy.

I remember the day I phoned my doctor to see if he had the results. I was at work at the Value Drug Mart in Fairview. (We had not told anyone that I was pregnant)

When my doctor told me that the baby was healthy and there was no evidence of the disease, I was elated!!

I still had multiple ultrasounds throughout the pregnancy to keep us all at ease and on May 31 my second daughter Ahstyn was born.

Yes!!! I had a healthy baby!!

But now the dread set in. I suffered from PTSD from the loss of Jaidin, and I didn't realize how the loss still affected everything I did. From her first night, I could not let her sleep in the bassinet in the hospital. I couldn't move to get her (another C-section), and I was so paranoid that she would stop breathing (I held Jaidin in my arms when she passed away), so I held her next to me and slept. I did this till she was two, or maybe even three, and after that, she still slept in the same bed as me. I just couldn't handle the thought of losing another child; I had to be in control of her health. Even 13 years after her birth, she still likes to have a sleepover in my bed, and we watch movies and fall asleep.

I was a more protective mom from the previous loss, ask Ahstyn now and she will tell you that!

Every year on Jaidin's birthday, Ahstyn and I release a balloon into the sky or buy a stuffy that we set out and celebrate her birthday with. It's a pain that never goes away no matter how long it has been. That child is always a part of you, and you will always feel that loss, it may not look it on the outside but on the inside the hole is ever present.

BIO: *Tannis Soderquist*

Tannis Soderquist is a personal fitness trainer; she coaches her clients to be the best that they can be in fitness and health. She helps them to organize nutritional meals that help to maintain their ideal weight.

Tannis also has her own Life Insurance Business, and again she helps clients maintain their lifestyle with their financial needs.

Together with her daughter and long-time boyfriend Joey, they live in Alberta Beach on a small acreage with their dogs and cat.

Tannis hopes that in sharing her story about the loss of her first child, she will be able to provide some comfort to others who have and are going through it.

Girl, Interrupted

By Charlene Lumsden

*G*rowing up, I thought my tumultuous childhood was pretty normal as it was all I knew. What I have come to realize as I talked with more people about their lives and experiences, is that my normal childhood was a lot more "normal" than society has dared to acknowledge or admit up until now.

Since I became aware that being sexually abused was part of my childhood experience, I haven't talked much about it. I've since realized that keeping silent doesn't help in healing and moving forward; and, abuse thrives in silence. I have chosen to share some of my story with the hope that we can reduce the occurrence and alleviate the impact that sexual abuse has and help others to move forward and heal from this trauma. It's a privilege and honor sharing some of my story and journey with you.

Even though I currently have no conscious memory of the abuse I encountered from my father, I do know because of associated recollections and feelings, that it started for me at a much younger age than the pre-teen/teenage years of my eldest sister. These memories are from the time and the house that our family lived in from when I was ten months old, until the summer before my 8th grade in school, at age twelve.

I remember knowing which stairs creaked in the climb to our bedrooms upstairs. I also developed the skill of being able to identify people by the sound of their walk before even seeing them. With six children in the family, we often shared a bedroom, especially the younger ones. One of the bedrooms I eventually had to myself was the middle room at the top of the stairs.

From upstairs one could see the red CN light on top of the tower downtown, and I had a particularly good view sitting on the overhang outside my bedroom window. As it switched from side to side, I found particular comfort in the consistency and reliability of the light as I sat and watched it from my little peaceful retreat. One time while out there, my father had come looking for me and found me in my solitude on the awning.

He said, "Oh, you're out there," and asked if I was coming in.

When I didn't come in, he didn't wait around for me to do so. I'm sure if he had it wouldn't have been to read me a bedtime story. I do remember my two older sisters playing a nurturing role with me and reading at night, often until I fell asleep, resuming the story the next night. Perhaps their way of doing what they could to keep me safe.

Another memory of my father is a time that we were out at a family event, and I was tired and fell asleep in the car on the way home. My father carried me from the car up to my bedroom, and in the process, I woke up, though I pretended to be still asleep. In leaving me in my bed, he said, "Oh, you're asleep, are you? Oh, okay."

To this day, my father does not express any guilt or remorse in his life and actions.

At the age of 91, during a recent hospital admission, he said that he hasn't done anyone any harm and that those who think so are mistaken. This perception was evidenced by another interaction we had in my early family home. My parents had a flip clock at their bedside before the advent and popularity of digital technology. I was eager to see the clock flip to 11:11, as I felt it was special because there was no other time where one number or the number one, appeared four times. Usually, I was at school during the day or in bed at night when that occurred, so the opportunity to see it never seemed to arise.

One evening I was up late, and my parents were out or busy, so I thought if I could stay up a little bit longer, this might be my chance. As going into their bedroom was neither encouraged nor permitted, I was taking a chance. I entered the forbidden zone of my parents' room, and while watching the clock and waiting for it to hit 11:11, I fell asleep.

Sometime later my Dad came to bed and seeing me there responded with, "Oh, you want it bad, do you?"

Reflecting on this now sickens me and helps me to understand why I, just like so many other boys and girls who experienced abuse, grew up with such distorted ideas about ourselves, about love, sex, sexual identity, and boundaries.

Not knowing when the abuse started, or for how long it lasted doesn't seem relevant to me at this point because I know the results it has produced and the lifelong struggle to change, and overcome the impact and beliefs growing up in a home of abuse has had. My perception was clouded in terms of how, and what it means to be female in this world, of what was right and normal in sexual relationships, of what to expect from others, of beliefs about myself, my value and worth, and of my capacity to contribute, and offer back to others and the world.

As children growing up in our family we were expected to sit quietly, behave ourselves, be seen and not heard: if only rarely seen. Something my mom has said was her experience growing up as well. Being invisible was safer too because attention meant abuse and shame which resulted in me wanting to shrink, or run and hide.

If I could fly under the radar and not be seen or noticed, maybe the abuse would stop. I'm not sure if I told anyone about it, or if I buried it in my mind to cope. Or perhaps, if it happened young enough to be part of my normalcy, I didn't feel that this was something that warranted talking about. It was certainly not something that was talked about in our immediate or extended family.

Mom's take on it was that she knew or heard about Dad's impropriety with other family, and neighborhood women, but never dreamed it would happen with his own children. She also said that she didn't understand why he would look elsewhere when he was getting it every day at home.

My family's modus operandi has been to shove the secrets and indiscretions to the recesses of silence, and cover that with the look of normality. This sense of keeping up appearances was brought to my attention by my sister. If everything looked perfect on the outside—perfect home, kids dressed perfect, clean and well-behaved, then no one would notice the ugliness that was going on behind closed doors. Those beliefs, programs, and operating systems run deep, and I still see how they play out in my life.

I learned that I didn't matter. My value was based on how I looked on the outside, and how my home looked. Home wasn't a safe place, and there was no one there to protect me; I wasn't worth protecting. I wasn't acknowledged or heard. I learned that my voice didn't matter. It was best to keep quiet. My silence molded me into an introvert. I learned and believed that there must be something wrong with me.

Anger was something that developed from not being heard, and I remember slapping a girl in elementary school on the stomach and feeling such remorse afterward. Growing up we went to church, as it was the right thing to do, and I learned that anger was not an accepted or righteous emotion. I remember numerous times my mom mentioning that when I became a Christian as a child, that I was no longer angry. The reality was that I stuffed the anger further down and a put on a bigger mask. Without a healthy perception or outlet, the anger became sadness, and I grew up with the nickname of "Cry-baby." Crying was ridiculed and also not an accepted emotion.

So many of my perceptions were clouded, and the full expression of me, and my emotions as a little girl, and as a woman were stifled. Children were expected to behave like adults in the home, and in the bedroom. My childhood was interrupted.

Childhood curiosity was squashed. I went from a curious girl who had so much love to give, kissed everyone good night, loved to climb on top of everything and explore, to a girl who sat quietly and had a fear of the future, and the unknown. The little girl in me was put away, only to be acknowledged, seen, and heard decades later.

As a young adult in high school and university, I felt less than adequate and not worthy or loveable. I was so thrilled when the man that I had dated in university asked me to marry him. Really?! Did someone love me enough to want to spend the rest of his life with me? I was over the moon!

My programming and beliefs marched on and eroded the marriage that limped along at times, with two broken people trying to feel better about themselves, eventually ending over twenty years later.

No longer did I have someone in my life that wanted to be with me. This gave me an opportunity for much reflection and threw me back into the chaos, uncertainty, and unworthiness I felt as a child.

From this place, I began my journey of self-discovery, and spiritual exploration. I started on a path of personal development, examined my beliefs, and learned about some of the things that have contributed to the choices that I have made in my life up until now. This has given me the opportunity to forgive my dad, my mom, my ex-husband, and most importantly myself. I have the awareness, tools, and belief that I do matter to others, and to God and that I do have value. I am not defined and limited by those who have responded to me out of their brokenness and beliefs. I've been able to break free from those chains and make my own decisions about who I am and my value. My value is founded and rooted in being a human being who is created and loved by God.

I have greater capacity than I have lived out up to this point, and I'm excited to wake up each day that God allows me to do that. I make better choices than I did before and forgive myself quicker than I did before, remembering that my value isn't dependent on what I do. I am free to create the life I'm meant to live, free from the things that have shaped and defined me. I have work to do. I have a voice and something of unique value worth saying. My victory can be someone else's inspiration.

Everyone has a unique purpose and unique giftedness, and I am excited about opportunities to help others to see and live that out, to open doors for others and lead them to a better future that is free from the chains of the past. I am doing that for myself by removing from my life and my beliefs, the definition of others, redefining myself, and discovering and living out the purpose that I am here for. I am rediscovering the truth about myself that I had lost sight of.

I am writing my story.

Every day is a new chapter, and I can and am making new choices. I allow love into my life by receiving and giving love because, I am loveable, and I love myself.

The biggest evidence of this in my life is starting my own business. Putting myself out there and taking a risk wasn't how I used to be. Playing it safe and not living out my impact was what I used to do. Another example was on our way to a recent annual convention. I wore a black, form-fitted dress with orange and yellow flowers. It was a big departure from the oversized or baggy mono-chromatic darks that were more characteristic of me. This happened to catch the eye of a gentleman we traveled with, because, I'm sure, of my confidence and warm presence.

After the convention, we connected, and when he suggested we go for a drink, I took a big gulp and said, "Sure." It is so great to say yes: to that first encounter, to having someone in my life and to not living in distrust or feeling like I'm waiting for the other shoe to drop. I deserve to have someone amazing in my life who thinks the world of me. So many times I see circumstances, from our first kiss, to have those difficult conversations, where I recognize that I'm living in the present and not in the past and that I can trust myself. I've got this. And, I can trust someone else to have my best interest at heart.

It is a journey that I take one step at a time, knowing that God is with me every step of the way and has always been. I hope that others would have the courage to walk with me and take their next step in moving beyond the challenges they have encountered, not letting those stop or define them, but rather using them as catalysts in becoming the people that we were meant to be.

BIO: *Charlene Lumsden*

Charlene is the youngest of six children in her family. After enjoying the lower mainland of BC for nine years where she married and received a Bachelor of Arts Degree in Physical Education, she moved with her husband back to Edmonton, her city of birth. She recently transitioned from a career helping people rehabilitate their health, to a career where she supports people in bettering their current and future financial situations.

Charlene received her life licensing through the Alberta Insurance Council and completed the Canadian Investment Funds Course to obtain her securities license through the Mutual Funds Dealers Association.

Passionate about making a difference in and improving the lives of others, she is thrilled to be able to educate and teach her clients and associates about effective financial solutions and strategies for personal growth.

Outside of work she is quite active in the community, volunteers for various organizations, and enjoys creative expression through arts and music.
Associate
World Financial Group
4803 87 Street NW Suite 12 Edmonton AB T6E 0V3
780-229-3356 https://howmoneyworks.com/charlenelumsden
www.wfgconnects.com/charlenelumsden

Courage to Heal

By Sheryl Rist

On Friday, the start of my boys' weekend with their dad, Anthony stood in front of his computer screaming that he was not going. He didn't want to be lectured again. Yet only 5 minutes before this outburst, he had been happily drawing. My simple act of telling the boys it was time to go to their dads was all that was needed to unleash a screaming banshee. After the screaming banshee was set off I needed time to compose myself and went for a few breaths in the kitchen. At exactly that moment my other son Steven, attempting to escape his brothers screams, breezed by so fast that he spilled orange juice all over the floor.

Since the screaming fit, I have cleaned the floor, received a half a dozen threatening emails from the ex, fed the boys, woke Anthony up from a nap, and calmed everything down to the point of finally dropping the boys off at dads. Chaos breaks out quite easily when you are a single mom with twin boys going through a divorce with a narcissist.

Any part of that sentence above can cause immediate, unmistakable chaos of the highest order: single mom, twin boys, divorce, and narcissist. All these together, and pandemonium reigns on a regular basis. It has taken me the last two years to be able to manage the difficulties so that life can function semi-normally. It has also taken me two years to be able to understand what narcissism is and how the abuse affects others, including children.

I love being a mom. There is nothing I love more in the world. When I was new into the dreamy part of the relationship with my ex I was very happy. Happy enough, to consider becoming pregnant and having children with him. The American dream of a family and white picket fence reared its unmistakable head. Mesmerized by the hypnotic stare of the dream, I searched for ways that I could have children.

Being forty-two years old and all, I checked out adoptions and IVF. I went through the tests of having iodine pushed through the fallopian tubes, looking for a way out when none was available, and as a result, I knew the only way this girl was having children was through IVF. So the question became: should we try once to have children the IVF way or be DINKs forever? The Double Income No Kids life did have its appeal. I was on the fence, and my husband talked me into giving IVF the good old college try. So I did.

The universe decided that once was all it took—one time with only five eggs at the elderly age of 42. All five eggs were fertilized, all five eggs were put inside me, and two decided to grow.

Excited, I wanted everyone to touch my belly. I couldn't believe I was going to be a mom. I couldn't believe that I was going to have two boys. I was so ridiculously happy. I was going to be a big-bellied mom with twin boys and lots of love to give. I didn't realize that my happiness was to be short-lived.

My wonderful husband, who had stood beside me while I got injections for IVF, now wouldn't even touch my stomach to say hello to his boys. He started smashing items around the house, yelling and swearing at me. He threw water bottles at my head and called me names, saying I was going to be the worst mom ever. I thought it was his nerves. I thought he was just a hesitant dad.

At the same time, I started to get really big. I had a 26-inch waist before, and now it was almost forty-seven inches. Most women have constipation with being pregnant; I had diarrhea when I walked very far. I was becoming more vulnerable the more pregnant I became. And the more pregnant I became, the more of an ass my husband was becoming. I prayed this would end soon. I did not realize this was the beginning of the end of our beautiful brief marriage.

I was angry. It wasn't just the hormones, although I am sure they did not help. I was angry because of how I was being treated. I felt like I was the only one who had signed up to become pregnant and I was dragging a ferocious grizzly bear behind me. We almost lost the house, we almost lost each other, and I had to work longer than intended. I was angry because my wonderful husband was having a temper tantrum at me being pregnant. It didn't make sense to me.

Finally, the boys were born, and I was sure this would change everything. Steve would see how great it was to be a dad, and I could have the American Family dream I had wanted. Stupid American Family Dream! For those of you, who have been through this already with a narcissistic ex-spouse, please feel free to laugh and skip to the end of the next paragraph. You've already been through enough. I now understand the sad irony of it.

I decided to continue with life and to love my little boys as much as I could. Steve's actions and attitude only got worse. At the same time, I tried to move on with my career as an acupuncturist/doctorate of natural medicine. Each time I started to get ahead, the craziness in the house would be ramped up until I had no choice but to slow down my job, quit my present opportunity, stop trying to progress and come back to that which meant the most to me—my children and my family.

Then I would be blamed for the finances being tight, for not enough money to get ahead, and the fact that I was unable to hold down a job. This is the narcissistic way: make life so difficult that changes have to be made and accommodations applied, and then blame the other person who has just lost out on their opportunity. Experts call it "crazy making."

Everything always happened in front of the children. This was my weak time as I didn't want the children to see either their dad like this or their mom being treated in such a nasty way. All threats, yelling, insults, all abuse happened in front of the children. When the children weren't there, I was living with Mr. Wonderful. When the children were there, peace was not to be found. No one believed me of course. Mr. Wonderful outside the home, Mr. Loved-by-all outside the home. But in the home, that was a different story.

Steve's actions started to become physical after a couple of years. In truth, this was a blessing for me because I wouldn't stand by and have my children watch their mom be hurt by their dad. Since everything always happened in front of the children, it did not take long before I was before a judge looking for a restraining order.

At first, after Steve was removed from the house, I did not know what to do. It was surreal. I was able to be in my home and be free—think my own thoughts, treat the boys the way I wanted to. Fix things that were broken. I felt so free and so allowed. My children and I danced in the morning, danced at night, sang and jumped and played, and had the time of our lives. Then it hit me. I did not know who I was anymore.

Everything I had stood for before the marriage seemed trivial. Everything I had become during the marriage was a result of survival mechanisms. I had lost myself, and now I had two boys to bring up as well. I didn't know what to do, what I liked or who I was anymore. I began to realize that something had really happened to me, spiritually and emotionally.

Around that time I met up with a mortgage broker. She took one look at me and informed me that I reminded her of herself a few years ago. She believed that I had been "narcissistically abused."

"How do you know?" I asked, warily. "Because," she said, "I was you."

We talked, and she presented me with meditations specific to narcissistic abuse and links to information. At first, I did not believe what had happened. However, as I read and learned more, it became very clear. My ex-had all the same traits as a classic narcissist. I started on the meditations and did them every day for months. To this day, I still use them.

It's now been three years, and I've never looked back. Every day I know that I did the right thing and made the right decision for myself and my children. Every day I heal a bit more.

This doesn't mean chaos still does not rear its ugly head. Such as the event I have just been through with Anthony. Dealing with a narcissistic ex is an experience unto its own. I am sure my name has been slurred by the countless stories he told to others of how I have mistreated our children to the extent that they lay on the ground starved, thirsty, and beaten out of all their dreams. Of course, this is far from the truth. However, I am sure this is how he would like me to be seen, because it makes him feel worthy and maybe people will look at him as if he is the hero of this tragic story.

So yes, life can be hard. Life can be trying. Is it worth living? More than ever. Can one heal from wounds so large they become craters of the soul? Depends. We can furnish the craters created by the abuse and live in them. I tried that for a while. Or, we can choose to stand in the middle of the crater and do the hard work of releasing that which does not belong to us, until we rise to the surface as our true self-filled with appreciation, forgiveness, awe, and universal love.

I didn't and couldn't have done this hard work on my own. Meditations, nutrition, and supplements have allowed me to become the person I am today. I am thankful for all the help so many people have given me. How I dealt with the narcissist made a big difference for me, so I'm also grateful for my courage and strength.

I am grateful for my boys. I take courage and stand up for them because they gave me the courage to heal. They are my greatest gifts in life.

I hope that with my story, I give you the courage to heal and the trust that the universe will support you.

BIO: *Sheryl Rist*

Everyone today goes through trauma of some type. Everyone has their stuff to deal with, some more than others. Some become bitter about it, and some eventually look at their trauma as a blessing and use it to help and heal others.

Sheryl believes that she must have signed up for the trauma train when she came into this lifetime. Sheryl believes that she has been blessed, as with each trauma comes life experience, or "character" as her Mom use to say. She is now able to take each of these valuable lessons and help others come out of the dark tunnel into the field filled with sunshine and life.

Dr. Sheryl Rist business is to help people become healthy after trauma. Balanced Lifestyle and Wellness was created to help people balance wellness with their lifestyles.

Dr. Rist is an acupuncturist and has her doctorate of natural medicine. She understands how trauma affects the body and what is required to bring it back into alignment. Dr. Rist loves what she does and is thankful that this continues to be a part of her life path.

Here and Now!

By Tenshy Perdomo

"Sometimes you will never know the true value of a moment until it becomes a memory."

Many years ago, when I was younger, more naive and pure, I gave my heart to a lovely boy. I didn't know how much his presence in my life was going to mean to me. I still can remember the first time I saw him in the elevator of the building I had recently moved into. I was going from the fourteenth floor to the lobby, and the elevator stopped at the first floor where he lived. He looked at me, clearly checking me out, and I looked back at him like, "What's wrong with you?"

He was older than me, and the brother of one of my new friends in the building. I was in my last year of high school, and let's just say that school was not my favorite place to be. I wanted to move on to other adventures. Towards the end of the school year, many celebrations were happening: fairs, concerts, performances, and other events that I was more interested in then what was happening at school.

One day, I was on my way to one of these events, coming out of the building through the underground parking, which I hadn't ever done before. But that day I did, and I saw this "angel" walking towards me-the boy from the elevator. I don't know how to describe it, but it felt like something important was happening when I saw him that day, almost like there was a bigger plan, a divine plan for us. I remember thinking "what was that?" But I wouldn't know until a short while later.

At this point I already knew his name, J.J. It had turned out that everyone in the building knew him, since he turned twenty; he was diagnosed with a congenital condition that made his heart twice as big as it should be.

J.J. was a lively person, who never acted sick; he was kind-hearted and so funny! When his heart's health began to decline, his activities out of the home were limited. He had to withdraw from some university classes, and spend more time under the care of his mother, as well as welcoming visits from his friends.

In Venezuela, where I'm from, people, especially family and friends, are close to each other. We're predisposed to help and take care of each other, especially those less fortunate.

Knowing about J.J.'s heart condition motivated my group of friends to visit J.J. on a regular basis. During the end of my last year of high school, I started to visit J.J. on my own, growing this friendship into something else, until I fell in complete love with this being whose heart needed way more than my love.

By fall of the same year, the companionship and the love of his family and friends made J.J. stronger, enabling him to go back to University, which was, of course, the same university I chose to attend.

Our days together began early in the morning, with him picking me up at my house and driving together to university. I was in my first year studying education, and he was in his third year of Engineering, two different worlds, which never seemed to be a problem for two lovebirds. I remember telling my parents I had classes all day long, copying his class schedule so I could be there with him for longer hours!

We made a life together, despite my family's advice against it, given his age and the risk my heart took in falling in love with a person whose heart and life was uncertain. Our days together grew longer and longer, J.J. spending more time with my family and me. We went to everything together-reunions, social events, or even just the movies. It was like being married, without the actual document.

In the spring of 1999, J.J.'s health took a turn for the worse. He needed heart surgery as soon as possible, and the quest to find the doctor and the financial means for him to get it began, and "Un Corazón Guerrero-A Warrior's Heart" Foundation was created.

The doctor who could operate resided in Curitiba, Brazil, and J.J. needed to get to him, not the other way around. To cover all of the expenses, J.J. needed $50,000.

The money came from every pocket possible, from people donating on the streets of Caracas, from the University we attended, from family and friends, and through concerts and artist's performances dedicated to the cause.

In July 1999, after school was done, my parents gifted me with an airline ticket to accompany J.J. and his mom to Curitiba, Brazil.

So many people came to say goodbye and wish him good luck. We couldn't wait to be done with the surgery and to come back home. On our return home and after his recovery, wedding plans awaited us, as J.J. had asked my parents for permission to marry me.

We were inseparable. I constantly thought we were a puzzle made of only two pieces. I bathed, fed, helped him with his clothes, and paid attention to what he ate, his medication, his restful moments, and more.

Once we arrived in Brazil, we went to the hospital, where the surgery was scheduled for the very next day. We had known that traveling had included the risk of blood clots, among other things, as his heart was already the size of a watermelon.

We had a long night of prayers and meditation, repeating the same healing mantra for hours and hours, hoping for this surgery to be the answers to our prayers: J.J. having a healthy heart, me marrying the man of my dreams, and us living happily ever after.

At 5:00 in the morning, the nurses came into the room to wake us up; they had to get him prepared for his open heart surgery. The surgery was going to replace his mitral valve with another.

The fear I'd been working so hard to push down, resurfaced and my heartbeat felt like it was going a 100 kilometers per hour.

The language barrier (Portuguese-Spanish) also didn't help me understand exactly what was going on, which was also stressful.

After the nurses prepared him for surgery, J.J.'s mom and I walked toward the operating room when I suddenly realized something: I didn't hug him! I quickly thought I'd hug him later, I'll hug him tomorrow, but for me, tomorrow and later never happened.

J.J. died on a rainy July day in 1999, at the age of 22. Doctors found his heart was in a state worse than they'd ever imagined. He left three brothers, his mom and dad, and a bride to be, all with broken hearts.

I fell into total depression, desperation, anger and rage, all at the same time. I felt completely abandoned. I was mad at him for leaving me alone, mad at God for taking J.J. to be with him, mad at the doctors, nurses and everything and everybody for what was happening to me.

The night he died, his mom and the doctors agreed I shouldn't see his body, so I never got to say a proper goodbye. I remember the last words I said to him: "Remember, you have to make me the mom of three children." To which he'd agreed with a nod of his head.

After going back to Venezuela with his body in a coffin, my family helped with the funeral arrangements and prepared to deal with my broken heart.

I really can't remember those days very well. I know I had to take some medication to help me cope with the loss of my fiancé. I'd become almost a widow' at the age of nineteen, and I promised him, and myself that I would never love anyone else like I loved J.J.

The days passed, and my use of medications lessened every day. My family and friends all took turns staying with me overnight, so I would never be alone, and to prevent me from doing something crazy to hurt myself. They tried everything to distract me from grief: movies, music, trips to the beach. My parents even took me on a cruise ship to the Caribbean to get me out of my deep sadness.

As time went on, I started to re-awaken my God-given gift: awareness of and connection to the spiritual world. This gift used to be present when I was a child and I could "hear" voices saying things about my family and family members as well as "know" when things were just about to happen and have that sense of knowing. It allowed me to "know" when J.J.'s spiritual energy was anywhere in the room. I could 'feel' when this energy was near my bed, holding my hand, walking next to me, or just sleeping next to me. One night, after my nightly ritual of writing J.J. a letter about my day, I fell asleep and woke up in the most mystical dream I'd ever had.

I was on a misty island, surrounded by nature, and lots of trees. There was nobody else in that place but me. No animals, no birds, no other human beings around. I couldn't tell if it felt cold, hot, moist or dry.

But it felt like another piece of land was moving next to the trail I was walking on. I continued walking, and to my right appeared a hanging bridge. I decided to walk on it, and as I went further, I noticed J.J. walking towards me, coming from the other piece of land.

My eyes couldn't believe what I was seeing. I rushed to get to him, and standing in front of him I asked him crying, "Why did you leave me? Why did you die? I can't live without you."

He responded, "I did not leave you. I'm always with you, your heart and mine are a puzzle of only two pieces. I just came to hug you."

After I awoke from that dream, my entire body was vibrating. I felt as though I had sat on a working engine. Vibrating more and more. I could not move, and even breathing was painful and hard.

This whole experience led me to a spiritual quest, one I'm still on right now.

I'll always remember something a stranger said to me that night J.J. died. When J.J.'s mom and I went to our hotel to spend the night, I remember crying at the entrance, looking at the bright sky that had been dark and pouring earlier. Wondering how the stars could shine on a sad night like that one.

A man walking by stopped in front of me and, without even knowing who I was or what I was thinking about, in his plain Portuguese said, "I know that you are sad. And I know how you feel, but you have to know that your heart and his heart, will always be together."

He continued, "If you are sad, he is sad. If you are happy, he is happy."

I didn't know who that man was. It was our first night at that hotel, and J.J. was already gone. But for me, this was a walking angel who gave me a reason to remember that J.J. was still with me.

That message made me keep the promise I made to my beloved J.J. and myself on the way back to Venezuela: "I will live happily for you and me.

Every experience I have will be for you and for me. I will be your eyes, your ears, your nose and your hands. My heart will be your heart, and I will live every moment to the fullest. Because I will be living for me, but also for you."

J.J.'s death brought so many gifts to my life that I really wouldn't be able to list them all here. My spiritual awareness is, without a doubt, the biggest of all, followed by the ability to live presently, in the here and now. It has made me the woman who won't wait for tomorrow or later to go and savor the world.

It has made me a risk taker, a passionate lover, and a present mother. Always remembering that the best time of my life is now, and that I have a healthy body. That the best time of my life is now that I have my man next to me. That the best time of my life is now that I am finally the mom I've always wanted to be. All of this for him, and for me.

My bond with J.J.'s spirit and also with his family is still alive today after so many years. That part of my story is one of the hardest ones, but also one of the experiences that has shaped me into the strong and resilient woman I am today.

I'm forever grateful to life, and to God for showing me the other side, in which I have had the pleasure to be many other times, but that is a story for another time.

BIO: *Tenshy Perdomo*

Tenshy Perdomo was born and raised in Venezuela and grew up with her parents and three siblings. Graduated from University with a degree in Early Childhood Education, and worked as a preschool teacher and a Jr. Kindergarten teacher for nearly 20 years.

In 2004 moved to Canada where ten years after, the birth of her son Nicolas led her to connect with her real purpose in life: becoming a better version of herself, and better role model for her son. She aims to inspire other mothers wanting to change the world, by changing the way they raise and think about their children and themselves.

As a yoga instructor for children and adults, Tenshy practices mindfulness daily, by living and valuing every present moment, knowing that moments will become memories tomorrow. This has led her and her husband Ivan to open and operate Family Filmmaker, a video production company devoted to families who value their moments and want them captured for generations to come as a way of leaving their legacy.

Silver Lining

By Jordan Guildford

*M*y childhood was riddled with lies, tragedy, confusion, and heartbreak. Although many obstacles befell me, I had unwavering belief I would one day be financially fortunate, marry my prince charming, and have every dream realized. These beliefs paid off, not because of faith in myself, but because I learned to silence the doubt, and focus on my dreams, they were my ultimate 'silver lining.' The thing about dreams is that no one can take them away from you. Over time, I realized that through routine focus, my dreams became achievable goals. Once realized, this process shaped every aspect of my life.

As a child I was happy. I defaulted to always looking for the "silver lining" to unfavorable situations. I was hopelessly naive and was frequently (and lovingly) made fun of by my family for how trusting I was. My love of family, sports, animals, my friends and every opportunity to socialize were the epicenters of my universe. I was home-schooled from grades six through nine, which made time with friends even more precious.

At fourteen years old, I was head altar-server at our church. I trusted, grew close to, and was subsequently sexually abused by our parish priest. Life as I knew it, ended.

I struggled to find something to be able to maintain my happiness, a way to reconcile my deep belief in the fact that priests are categorically 'good people,' with what was happening. I needed a silver lining to default to.

This was the beginning of the focus on my dreams. Each time, almost every Sunday after mass, for a year, I would focus on feeling sad for him and imagining a beautiful picture of the life I would have as a woman. It was a confusing and ultimately, very lonely time for me.

At the time the Catholic Church was getting a lot of press about covering up stories regarding abusive Priests. In our small parish, "keeping the faith," victim shaming, and attention seeking were hot topics among the "faithful." Since my family was devout, I didn't feel brave enough to speak up and potentially be lumped in with the "attention seekers" category or worse, to have the spotlight shone on me, and ultimately not be believed.

The priest used words like "love," and gave me compliments I'd never heard before. They weren't those of a boy to a girl, rather of a man to a woman. He struggled with himself, and I saw that. I knew it was wrong, but because I could see his sadness, I didn't want to make things worse for him by exposing what was happening. I also didn't fight, and this confused me.

I knew I had zero interest, and I knew I hated it, and didn't want it at all. Because of what came out of his mouth, his gratitude, and sadness for the woman he loved and gave up to "follow his calling" into the priesthood, the fact that I reminded him of her as a young woman, etc., all made me feel so sad for him. I often asked for it all to stop, for it to end and for him to leave me be, but when he pushed, I let it happen. Limp, unresponsive, both of us dreaming of another time.

After a year, he retired and moved away. Within weeks we were given a new priest, a younger one. I was terrified he had knowledge of what I had been enduring for a year and consequently, would expect the same thing. He would graze my breasts as he reached for my necklace, or collar of my top, making excuses like really liking dolphins (my necklace charm), or that there was something on my top, etc. For months I thought it was only a matter of time before he'd take up where his predecessor left off. I'm relieved to say he didn't.

Two years later, I became 'brave' enough as a sixteen-year-old, to speak up and tell an adult what had happened. I believed the only place truly confidential was in confession, and therefore with our priest. I explained the whole thing and was met with silence followed by a cringe-worthy response which I took as gospel and clung to for many years to come.

I was told that "…the devil is working through you to tempt good men. He is using all the gifts God has given you for evil. I have felt the devils pull through you and have struggled with it. You need to stay away from men. Particularly those who are committed (to God or another person), for five years, and pray that God gives men the strength to be strong against the Devil's work. It isn't your fault, but it isn't theirs either."

My head was spinning. I nodded and said nothing while choking back tears. I felt confused about where my worth lay, shame in the realization I was a vessel of evil, fear, more shame, and guilt filled my thoughts. It was past what I could handle, and consequently, I gave more and more focus on my perfect future to escape my current reality.

Another two years passed, I was now finishing my first year of university and that spring, I met my Prince Charming. The summer was filled with falling more and more deeply in love and living on my own for the first time.

It all came to a crashing halt in August when he left for football training camp. I believed we would marry one day, and he echoed that belief. The heartbreak I experienced when he left, ripped my heart apart. This relationship had redefined anything I had ever known of love to that point, and for the first time, I had a connection with someone truly there for me.

A month after he left, I went out with my childhood best friend, went back to the home of the guy she was seeing, and his friend raped me downstairs while they were upstairs. This time, I fought as hard as I could. To no avail. I passed out, and woke up hours later, and left. That old familiar feeling came flooding back in. Shame, worthless, evil and ultimately self-disgust.

The year after, I found out my best friend had heard what was going on downstairs that night but had no idea what to do, so, she did nothing. Again, isolation kicked in. It was very hard for me to connect to others in any way other than superficially. Around boys/men, I struggled to remain calm, even with others present. When I would occasionally find myself alone with a male, I couldn't breathe properly and would trip over whatever words I was able to get out. I avoided it whenever possible.

My boyfriend was kind, patient and incredibly understanding but it would take days for us to be intimate when we were able to see each other. In our long-distance relationship, our entire visit was only ever a few days. I frequently panicked when he hugged or held me. My psyche shouted, "You're Trapped!" "Run!" "You are vulnerable," "Unsafe!" etc. He was left hurt and sad, but above all, furious it happened in the first place.

I spent the next four years living with the reality of feeling worthless and cheapened by the "lesson" I had learned about my self-worth through being used and "allowing" myself to be so. I felt this way even with my family who, without knowing what had taken place, labeled my behavior, thoughts, and personality in general as "fluffy."

My focus on the future resulted in almost zero daily presence/care in current events. I isolated myself and made it very difficult for him to relate/speak to me about anything outside of that which they deemed "superfluous" (dreams, relationships, etc.) My instinctive behavior created a distance between us which made that time even harder. At the time, I didn't see what was happening.

Despite my inability to cope well with anything more than basic interactions with men, and the isolation from my family, my focus on working toward a beautiful future successfully kept me existing happily, well balanced, and excited for what life would bring. I would daydream many times, every single day about everything I wanted from life.

Sometimes, this would mean focusing on what my day would look like as a stay at home mother, (volunteering for charity, being fit, attending all events my children were involved in, etc.). Other times it would be in the relationship I wanted as a married woman, (strong communication, loving, teammates, committed, affectionate and kind). I focused on balance in all areas, and where I was unbalanced, I worked hard to create it through activity, relationships, work, and family.

After so many years this practice became a pastime, a hobby, a calling, and a way of living. Occasionally thoughts and old feelings would creep into my reality.

For instance, when people use rape as a joke around me, there would always be and still is, a moment that aches, and in that instance, I push it out. Later, it comes back, and I take a deep breath and intensely picture something I am excited about or would like. This is sometimes an amazing trip, a list of countries to visit, things I would like to accomplish before a certain age, etc.

When I turned twenty-four, a decade after I had first been abused, my Prince Charming, who had stuck by me through it all, asked me to be his wife. Upon marrying that wonderful man, the life I had focused on began to blossom. I felt safe for the first time in my life, and went from not just surviving, but thriving. The time I had been focused on came, and I was so very ready to make the most of life!

Through my struggles, I discovered that no matter what my personal beliefs were on religion, destiny, fate, good and evil, the most important thing was to have clarity on what you want to feel, see, and experience in life. This is the secret to experience, the benefits of manifesting/visualizing. You must invest yourself into the process. I focused on all things which made me happy because it was beautiful, in that beauty, I escaped, and in that escape, I committed to the process with all of myself. Positivity breeds positivity, and negativity also perpetuates negativity.

I discovered that only I choose which force my strength is given to and I chose positivity.

I am now married to a man who is exactly everything I dreamed of and have created two wonderful children with him. For the first five years of our marriage, I was a stay at home mother and very happily fully invested in that world. However, my experiences came to the surface once more as I grew stronger.

Feelings, thoughts, and ideas grew so loud in my head that I knew I needed to act. The desire to help women, who had been through versions what I had, was the base I used to make my calling a tangible movement. Two years ago, I founded a charitable movement called Gems for Gems which was created to empower women who have suffered and survived abuse. This was the final piece of my original dream becoming a reality.

If you had asked me as a child if my dreams would come true, the answer would have been a resounding yes. I live a life now of dreams realized and new ones being fostered daily. I know this reality is attainable throughout life as long as I continue to unwaveringly, say yes, and believe.

BIO: *Jordan Guildford*

Jordan comes from the small town of Scott's Bay in Nova Scotia, where she grew up with her sister and brother on a small hobby farm consisting of sheep, ducks, and horses. Her mother and father very much wanted them to have a simple and peaceful childhood.

Unfortunately, life did not go as planned. Jordan's family suffered greatly. Food, hot water, and other essentials were often a luxury. Despite all they endured, Jordan learned some valuable lessons about humility, kindness and compassion, truth, honor, and courage. These are the principles by which she lives her life, and which became the foundation of Jordan's charitable movement, Gems for Gems.

Quest for Happiness

by Kathy Smith

*I*t was a warm January night, and my husband, and I was standing outside on the deck of our acreage home. My breath caught in my throat as I saw the vehicles pull around the bend of large evergreens into our parking area: one, two, three. Two police cars and victim services. My stomach lurched, and I felt bile tickle my throat. I watched two police officers and two victim services volunteers get out of their vehicles and walk towards me.

I braced myself. "Do you know why we're here?" the female police officer asked.

My throat closed as I braced myself. "I think so," I whispered hoarsely.

I held my breath.

"It's about Lindsay," she said. I watched her thin lips mouth the words, "His body was found this morning in a bed at the Transit Hotel in Edmonton."

I flinched at the news and panic rumbled in my guts. Oh, my God. It had finally happened. The hard-won happiness I had built for my family after my divorce was now over.

"Do you want us to tell your children?" the woman officer asked. "No."

"Do you want us to come in with you when you tell your children?" "No."

"Do you want victim services to come in?"

"No."

They left, and I sobbed on my husband's shoulder as he quietly held me. I had to tell my four boys that their Dad, my ex-husband, had finally drunk himself to death.

In the living room, I gently shared the news with my boys. My thirteen-year-old started sobbing, and my eleven-year-olds eyes widened in shock. My nineteen-year-old turned white, and my twenty-two-year-old was stunned in disbelief.

On day three, all hell broke loose. The emotional dam broke open, and my boys and I reeled from the flood of emotions that threatened to sweep us away. I sobbed. We sobbed. Lindsay's death was a tragic slide into the darkest recesses of addiction. We wept for the husband and father whose own pain was as powerful as the pain he inflicted.

Old memories surfaced, and suddenly I was propelled back to twenty-five years ago.

On a hot August night in 1988, my roommate Diane and I went to see Bob Dylan live at the Toronto CNE, Canadian National Exhibition grounds.

We found our seat and glanced around at the growing crowd. We were chatting, when a man excused himself as he shuffled sideways in front of us. My radar perked up as I gauged his height: taller than my six-foot frame. He sat down next to me, and we began chatting as Diane tapped her toes to the music.

There was an instant connection between me, and this mysterious man that came out of nowhere: I learned he grew up in Edmonton, just minutes from my childhood home and that we knew dozens of the same people. We chatted excitedly while we drank the stash of airline-sized liquor bottles he pulled out of his socks. The husky haze of inebriation grew with our laughter. We both knew that our lives had just changed.

Soon we were like suction cups; madly in love and always together. Our courtship was every girl's dream: to be wooed by an admirer so powerful that he took your breath away. He was romantic and sweet, gallant and chivalrous. Over the next two years, our love settled deep into our souls.

We married, pledging our lives to each other just weeks before our first son was born, and after moving back to Edmonton, our second son was born. We were ecstatically happy. Mostly.

In the beginning, Lindsay only drank on weekends, and the first few years we had fun partying together. After our third son was born, the partying wasn't fun anymore, and when I refused to drink with him, Lindsay angrily called me "the party pooper."

During Alberta's oil boom, an opportunity for self-employment rose for Lindsay, and he began making more money and working fewer hours. The ease of finances and his extra time propelled his drinking into overtime.

As my loneliness deepened, a slow simmer of resentment grew in my belly. Every day there was an excuse to drink: watching sports, weekends, birthdays, the first day of spring, completing a big job and of course, the never-ending nights out with his buddies.

Looking back now, I see that my thoughts began to skew under the chaos of alcoholism, and our marriage became a dance of dysfunction. I began to manipulate him, and his drinking cycle. I knew when to ask for big-ticket items like new flooring for our home, and once, I angrily spent the same amount of money on new furniture as he spent on a lawyer for his drunk driving charge.

We couldn't afford either one.

During my fourth pregnancy, Lindsay began disappearing for days at a time. Sometimes I had money, and sometimes I didn't. I was a stay-at-home mom, and the feeling of powerlessness overwhelmed me. I was witnessing my marriage, my family and my life disintegrating before my eyes, and fear engulfed me.

I continually begged Lindsay to quit drinking. I tried everything: screamed, whined, and talked, threatened, seduced, and yelled. My words fell on ears of denial that cloaked him with protection and guaranteed his permanent suspension of reality.

Chaos in the house increased as sedate drunks turned to mean drunks and those into violent drunks. After an explosion of violence ended, the old Lindsay that I fell in love with would appear, and my heart would burst with hope. We danced the cycle of abuse again, and again, and again.

I was nine months pregnant with my fourth child, and my life was totally out of control. Somewhere deep inside of me, I knew there was a better life for my children, and I never gave up my burning quest for happiness. On the advice of my brother, I attended my first Al-Anon meeting. I went in full of fear and trepidation, and with hope. Hope that happiness was indeed, possible. I regularly attended Al-Anon for the next six years and cried for the first two years solid as I healed.

My sponsor taught me that the fingers of alcoholism are long, spidery tentacles that slowly and cunningly spread their destructive power to everyone involved. For those living with active alcoholism, the emotional strangulation is a slow, steady process that resembles insanity. I was going insane.

The decision to end my marriage was filled with pain and terror; I now had four young boys to consider. When I told Lindsay that I had filed for divorce, his denial kicked in, and he simply changed the subject.

Frustration seared my guts, and I wanted to scream at him and shake him awake. Instead, I lowered my head and silently cried.

The first time I called the police was a warm summer evening after he exploded in snarling violence. Eventually, the realization that he was losing his family sent his rage into epic proportions. His pain and panic spewed out like scorching lava, scalding everything in its path. I believe now that the pain Lindsay inflicted on us was matched only by his own tortured and powerless descent into the addiction.

Lindsay's rage was focused as tight as a laser beam on me, and over the next two years, I called the police hundreds of times as he continued to threaten to kill me. I waded through three criminal trials against him.

Food for my family came from community donations and government assistance. Neighbors collected cash from people we didn't know, and friends appeared to help us in droves. That Christmas brought a bounty of presents from every direction. I was humbled again, and again by the outpouring of humanity. And then, I'd listen to a death threat on the answering machine the next morning. The extremes in my life were staggering.

Lindsay's rage finally dissipated after the third criminal trial, and we began to speak guardedly to each other. He lived like a nomad in cheap motels, contacting us only between binges. Lindsay began to lose weight and hollowness commandeered his eyes.

Lindsay's self-loathing deepened as alcoholism strengthened its hold on him, and life became a series of new lows and unfulfilled promises. Again and again, our sons waited with excitement for his visit, only to be disappointed by his empty promises. I saw him hurting our boys, and it fueled my hatred. The chaos was relentless. I wished for a binge to start so he would disappear for days. If he did, the uneasy peace provided relief, and we could relax.

Along with the drinking, the cycle of addiction would bring on the post-binge feelings of remorse and shame that overwhelmed Lindsay. The times we talked left me drained and depressed; his pain was the most exposed on these phone calls when his self-hatred was the deepest.

We were all helplessly watching him kill himself.

His skin eventually turned to the color of grey decay, and he resembled a walking corpse. His hospital stays became more frequent, and I became more jaded. I no longer had the patience to hear about his latest abnormal blood count, or about the convulsion that hijacked his brain and turned his body into a withering rag doll. The emotional toll was too great, and I no longer allowed the boys to visit him. The only time Lindsay drove drunk with his boys was the last time they were ever allowed in his vehicle. Lindsay's world became smaller and smaller.

And then he died.

The boys and I felt shell-shocked for months after the tornado of alcoholism ripped our family apart. The spectrum of emotions swung far and wide, but the overwhelming emotion for our boys was helplessness at the incredible waste of a much-loved father.

My sons and I decided on a private service, just the five of us. We trudged through the snow into the forest behind our rural home and picked a beautiful tree to dedicate to Lindsay. We each wrote our own letter to him, and weeping, we read our goodbyes aloud.

Two months later I took a leave from work to be at home with my grieving boys. They needed me more than ever. We talked for hours about their dad, alcoholism, death, and family. I rotated my time to be with each of them individually, as they poured their emotions out to me. I called the boys' school and explained the situation, so when the boys went back, they were greeted with warmth and condolences. Eventually, their grief bursts lessened.

I was mistaken to assume life would be relatively stress-free without living with the chaos of active alcoholism. You can imagine my shock when I went back to work after nursing the boys' grief only to be fired. I had neither the energy nor will to pursue the termination legally. I had no fight left in me. I felt lost.

My body, however, had other plans for me. It was time for me to grieve. It was time to walk through the black hole of emotional pain and come out the other side cleansed. I knew it had to be done. With a belly full of toxic and swirling emotions of anger, hurt, guilt and grief, I began my healing. I started with writing my letter to Lindsay and screamed out my anger. Not the letter from Mom like the boys had heard during our private service, but the letter from Kathy, the hurt, and abandoned spouse.

Over the next two years, I saw different therapists, each of them gently guiding me into self-awareness. Layer by layer, I drilled down below my resentment to remember why I fell in love with Lindsay. I had to grieve him, our failed marriage and our dreams together. I began to understand the decisions I made, good and bad and began the long process of forgiveness.

My boys are all young adults now, and they have grown into caring and responsible men. The bond between my sons and I is stronger now that we've survived the storm together. They are wonderful, beautiful human beings.

I have the love of my wonderful husband, a kind and gentle soul who came into my life seven years before Lindsay died. Our relationship did not come easy, and we have worked hard to create a healthy, happy environment. Our commitment to our relationship and the patience we've promised one another has allowed us to explore our vulnerabilities safely. With his love and support, I had the courage to write my book.

My story.

The whole story.

As I penned my life, I realized the darkest times brought the greatest miracles. But ultimately, it was my mindset, and the action I took that paved the way for the miracles to happen. My never-ending quest for happiness was the dangling carrot that propelled me forward, and I learned that asking for, and accepting help is a strength; it demonstrates what is important enough to fight for.

For me, my boys and I were it.

BIO: *Kathy Smith*

An earlier version of Kathy Smith's story, "Never Give Up," originally appeared in the book "Standing Together," created by the Alberta Women's Shelters.

An entrepreneurial spirit at heart, Kathy produced her own publication for five years, which led to her writing her column for the Spruce Grove Examiner, Stony Plain Reporter, and HomeTown Living. That column, "This is Life," the musings of a single mother, ran for a year.

Currently waiting for a double hip replacement, Kathy's search for natural pain relief led her to discover cannabis. Kathy is now a cannabis consultant, and considered an expert in her field, providing guidance and education to others. Kathy currently teaches cannabis workshops and advocates for the plant's natural, medicinal benefits.

Kathy is happily married to her best friend, and husband, Kelly. Kathy and Kelly created a warm, loving home for Kathy's four boys, who are now handsome young men. Kathy is looking forward to welcoming daughters-in-laws and grandchildren into her family.

Cell/Text: 780-722-5748 Email:Kathy.kgraphix@gmail.com

Finding My Wings

By Carolyn Block

*B*utterflies are such unique and fascinating creatures. They go through magical transformations; growing, evolving and developing wings to fly. Just like each of us, we are born soft, sweet and innocent. As we grow and experience life, we stumble and make mistakes, it is from those mistakes that we learn to grow and develop wings of our own and learn to fly. This is my journey; where I find my wings.

I grew up on a large farm, raised on love and respect. My parents are two of the strongest, most compassionate, hard-working people that have ever walked this planet. I'm so honored to have them in my life. They have taught me so much and stood by my side while I've taken them through hell. They've shown me time and time again that when the life gets tough, the tough get going, and you never have to face it alone; family always takes care of each other. My older sister Karen has been my best friend since birth, with an unbreakable bond. So many times, when I couldn't find the strength to face life, Karen would insist that "Polish Princesses" like us don't ever give up, and she kicks my butt back into gear. Forever a hero to me.

Just out of high school I met my ex-husband Marty, and our son Joshua arrived a few years later. I fell in love with my son, at first sight, in one simple moment he captured my heart. My joy and the light of my life that has shone brightly and kept me fighting. My biggest regret in life is the pain I've caused Josh and my family during my hardships, but their love has never wavered.

However, things with Marty and I were not all sunshine and roses. We were just never meant to be. I tried my hardest, and stayed with him for years, even after I emotionally 'checked out' of the marriage.

Admittedly, he is an amazing father, and he stood by my side through my first battle with cancer.

Back in 2000, over the course of a year, I had developed several large lumps on my neck and lost roughly forty pounds. Originally misdiagnosed as a thyroid problem, the masses on my neck dramatically increased in size and doctor was prompted to perform an emergency biopsy. During the biopsy, my doctor made a shocking discovery, starting to curse and looked quite stunned. I overheard him exclaim that he couldn't believe he missed something. In my head, I'm thinking, "Um, hey-I'm still awake, and I can hear you." But I stayed silent, and the doctor finished the biopsy without ever explaining his statement.

Within days, I was diagnosed with Stage 2 Non-Hodgkin's Lymphoma. I was horrified and in complete shock. From that point on, my life would never be the same. Over the next eight months, I fought a battle with my illness, both physically and mentally, as I underwent chemotherapy. I had to fight with every ounce of strength I could muster, Joshua needed me. When chemotherapy had run its course, and after innumerable appointments, and a cyclone of emotions I felt might never end, my battle with cancer was over. I had triumphed.

A couple of years later, Marty took a job in Valemount, BC in hopes that a fresh start could breathe some life back into our marriage. I loved the mountains so much, and it was there that I truly felt at peace. Our marriage, however, was beyond saving; so, one morning I gathered up the courage to tell Marty that I could no longer continue living a lie. I was making my getaway, and with that, our marriage ended. I was developing my wings and finally learning to fly on my own. The experience was positively empowering, all I needed was Josh, and my world was complete.

Soon after, I grew close to a co-worker named Daryl. He had lost his vision at a young age and was considered legally blind. He was a tortured soul with a wild and crazy spirit. He loved to drink excessively and be the center of attention, but he wasn't a good drunk at all. Our friends couldn't stand being around Daryl when he was drinking.

Despite the negatives, our love was blind to the world, and I accepted Daryl for who he was. Joshua and Daryl however, never did see eye to eye, as Josh blamed him for the end of my marriage. Despite some animosity between the boys, eventually, we settled down as a family. After several years it was time for a change, and Daryl accepted a job in Pincher Creek, Alberta, and I would stay in Valemount with Josh until the end of summer, and then join Daryl. Josh, citing the need for change too, packed his bags to go live with his dad for a while, and when he left, my world came crashing down. For the first time in my life, I was alone, and it terrified me.

I started drinking, playing poker and staying out late, mostly to avoid being alone. Daryl, between jealousy, and the distance between us, started to spiral out of control. His drinking escalated and he fell back into drugs, losing his job shortly after that. Daryl moved to Calgary with his parents, and our relationship ended. Again, I found myself devastated, unable to cope. I was physically and mentally a wreck. Karen helped me pack up my home and moved me in with her. Several months passed, I then moved to Calgary and within a short time, found myself back with Daryl.

One evening Daryl and I had a friend over for dinner and drinks. Daryl was drinking heavily, as was I, and we let alcohol fuel the fire. A few short hours after dinner, our guest had enough drama and decided to leave. Things between Daryl and I continued to escalate, the last thing I can remember is going towards the stairs.

Then I recall waking up in hospital, confused surrounded by my family. Apparently, the day following my accident, my family was notified that I'd been taken to the hospital. I had undergone emergency lifesaving surgery on my brain, and that the outcome was unknown. My family came rushing down to Calgary. Daryl on the other hand didn't seem too interested in visiting me at the hospital; maybe seeing me like this was too much for him.

I barely remember much of the first few days after I awoke. I had been in a drug-induced coma and on life-support for several days. They had removed the right half of my skull due to excessive swelling. The fall had caused blood clots in my brain a subdermal hematoma. After coming out of the coma, I was in a state of extreme emotional turmoil. My confusion was only amplified by my hurt and anger. "What could be going on?" my thoughts raced searching for answers.

Not much of anything made sense to me; I was confused as to why I was in the hospital. Why did family surround me? Why did Josh look so confused, heartbroken, and mortified all in one? Although I had so many questions, I also knew that I wasn't ready to deal with the reality of the answers. I remember being adamant initially about the fact that the entire incident wasn't a big deal...not at all.

Several hazy and confused days passed. I was still heavily drugged and having unsettling hallucinations due to a codeine allergy. Life was crazy, or maybe I was going crazy. During my stay at the hospital, I was extremely paranoid, and the sights, smells, and sounds of the brain injury unit I was admitted to were only amplifying every negative emotion. It wasn't until I was able to physically stand on my own that I first l saw myself in a mirror. I looked like a monster! My face was swollen, my eyes looked dark and puffy, half of my long dark hair had been shaved off, the right side of my head was oddly shaped and a freshly-stapled 12-inch incision running from the front of my head to the back. I was mortified and in utter shocked. It was a wake-up call. This was serious.

My mind again struggled to piece the memories together. How could this have happened? And where the hell was Daryl? I remembered being with him that night, and that thing hadn't been good between us, but why wasn't he here by my side? He had come to visit on a few occasions, but there was something 'off' in his behavior and his continued absence only further intensified my anger.

Daryl's explanation of the events made no sense either, claiming that after I "fell" down the stairs. He was just going to leave me there to sleep it off, but my body was apparently all twisted up at the bottom of the stairs, and I was making awful moaning noises. He had the ambulance get me but did not go with me to the hospital. My initial ambulance report stated suspected domestic abuse.

The day I got home from the hospital, Daryl phoned my family, demanding they come pick me up immediately because he couldn't take care of me. He swiftly packed a suitcase for me and sent me off to my mom, and Karen. Days later, Daryl broke up with me again, citing an unwillingness to be with a woman with short hair. Again, I was disgusted and shocked. I felt like I had been thrown out like the trash and emotionally crippled as a result. Even a blind man couldn't even find me attractive.

After a couple of months of despair, Karen stepped in and helped me take control of my life. She had cut my hair, held me up, and convinced me that I had a future. Shortly after that, I had a second surgery to replace the missing piece of my skull. In the weeks leading up to the surgery, I began to panic. My family desperately tried to reassure me and calm me, but it was not easily done at this point. I pushed through, and within a week or two, was returning to my old self. I was no longer mean and miserable. My energy levels returned, and I was finally ready to face the world again.

Daryl continued to make appearances, but things between us could never be the same. On one of Daryl's last visits, he introduced me to his friend Kelly, and we quickly became very good friends. A year later, I had morphed into a new life, like a butterfly-a new job, new friends. I even took a trip to Las Vegas and went skydiving, and for the first time, I felt in control. Kelly coming into my life was like the rainbow at the end of my storm, and the beginning of our amazing love story. I had finally found my true love and soul mate.

Life was going so well for several years when suddenly I was diagnosed with stage 2 cervical cancer and found myself once again fighting for my life. I was faced with a grueling combination of chemotherapy and radiation. My radiologist refers to it as the one-two punch. Well, it certainly knocked me on my butt hard. I fought back with every ounce of energy and determination I could find. I prevailed and kicked cancer's ass once again, with support from my family and friends.

To this point my life my path has its share of ups and downs. I would not change a moment of it. Of course, I've incurred a couple of battle scars along the way and had to repair my wings a few times. It's my journey, and I've done it my unique way. During which I've become the woman I am today. Loving, proud, happy…a survivor.

BIO: *Carolyn Block*

Carolyn grew up on a farm in central Alberta, the second of four children in a very close-knit family. Farm life taught her the value of hard work, respect, and discipline. At a very young age, Carolyn developed a passion for animals, nature, and travel. She enjoys camping, hiking and exploring our beautiful planet.

Carolyn's son, Joshua has been a great inspiration in her life and has inherited much of her sense of adventure. Often taking the road less traveled, and making cherished memories along the way.

Carolyn admits to being a bit of an adrenaline junkie, enjoying white water rafting, skydiving, and scary movies. She attributes it to the fact that she doesn't believe in fear.

Carolyn has one of her life's mottos tattooed on her arm, "what does not kill me, makes me stronger." Life has taught Carolyn that she is a true survivor and to live each moment to the fullest.

Secure in Love

By Susan Janzen

"The ache for home lives in all of us. The safe place where we can go as we are, and not be questioned."

*T*hese days I am secure in love. I wake up next to the man I have loved for almost thirty years. I look forward to each morning because he starts the tub and puts the coffee on and we sit in the Jacuzzi and just talk. My daughter calls me mid-morning to tell me about the latest accomplishments of my five-year-old sweet granddaughter and my grandson who is nearly two. My son calls me to tell me how much he likes his new job and updates me about his two small children. I get a few calls in the morning as I put together Real Estate deals for my happy clients and all these things bring me joy. The tears that I cry now are tears of gratitude. But my life wasn't always this happy and secure.

From the minute I was born, I was unwanted, neglected and abandoned. My mother loved me, I knew this in my heart, but I was in the way. I was keeping her from pursuing her dream of becoming a famous singer. So when I was a baby, she shuffled me off to live with strangers, this back and forth was my normal. When I was five years old I was living back home with my mom; I was home alone when there was a knock on the door. It was a lady from Social Services who said she was taking me away. I remember the feeling of panic and fear and asking if I could leave a note for my mom so she wouldn't worry about me.

I became a ward of the government and placed in a foster home where a teenage boy sexually abused me. This kind of attention was something I had never known and did not understand. I was afraid all the time. He would come into my bedroom each night, and I was too afraid to move and way too afraid to tell anyone. This went on for months, but as soon as I got the courage to call and tell my mom, she promptly came and took me out of that home. Unfortunately, I was immediately placed in another foster home where I was neglected, and where I had nightmares that woke me each night.

When I was eight years old, we moved to Edmonton, but it was not long until, at age nine, I was placed in a convent with 200 girls and six overworked nuns who took care of us. I remember sitting on the bench outside the front door each Sunday waiting for my mom to visit me. She would phone and say she was coming, but usually never did.

It was at this time that I starting going to the chapel. It was the only place that I felt safe. I asked to be baptized and began to rely more and more on my heavenly father, the father to the fatherless because otherwise, I was on my own. I remember praying, and I made a promise that I would finish school, get married before I had children and I was going to be a great mother. I prayed a lot and always asked for a large family who loved and accepted me. Although girls surrounded me, I was so lonely that I cried myself to sleep each night. Two and a half years later, mom took me home to live with her–I was twelve years old.

Mom suffered from mental illness and depression, but I knew that I could take care of myself. When I finished grade nine and was fifteen, I moved to Calgary where I lived with a great uncle and his wife and six children. I helped with the chores and took care of the children while I went to High School and also worked a part-time job.

As I got older, I understood why it was so difficult for mom to be the mother I so desperately wanted. Mom was put in an orphanage as a baby, and when she went home at ten years old, her mom had just given birth to her baby brother and handed the baby to my mom. She then kicked them both out of the house. Mom took care of the baby but was on the streets in Vancouver living on doorsteps and with people who took her in for two years before she was caught and forced to give up her baby brother—who was quickly adopted.

I know my mom did the best she could, and I forgave her for not being the mother that I wanted her to be. Still, that didn't stop the longing to be accepted with each new place and each new school, and the sensitivity to anything that even hinted of rejection. My childhood was full of insecurity—uncertainty about when my mom would come and take me away, anxiety about what would happen to me with each new placement, and fear that someone was going to hurt me.

I came back to Edmonton and finished high school. A promise that I had made to myself early on was not to drop out of school. I attended a total of 12 schools. I met a guitar player who was looking for a singer to join his band. We worked together as a duo, and yearning to be in a secure relationship, I married him, and we went on the road. We were booked solid on the road for five years and recorded an album. Life was good until I expressed a desire to stay home and have children.

Thinking that once we had a baby my husband would change his mind, was selfish and immature. My son was born the next year, and the day I went for my six-week checkup the doctor said, "Congratulations! You're pregnant!"

Even before my daughter was born, I knew the marriage was over. We had gone for counseling, but the lifestyle he chose was not healthy for me, or the children. He was putting my children in danger. We divorced in 1982, and I was on my own again. But this time I felt strong in the decision I made to protect and raise my children on my own. The children were two and three, and they were my priority, and I knew that the three of us would be fine. As a young mother, I found the strength that I needed and learned to be secure in loving myself and my precious children.

I quickly put a band together and had my calendar full of gigs. I applied to the Klondike Days Associate with 25 other women, 15 of us had interviews, and then I was shortlisted to the top 10 who auditioned. I won. I was the first local Klondike Kate. It was a big deal in the city, and I had a lot of press for two years. They asked me to audition for my second term, and I won again. I sang with Bobby Curtola here and in Las Vegas, worked with Lynn Anderson, Al Hurt, I met Mohammed Ali, and many other amazing entertainers and politicians. I did IGA and United Way commercials, television shows and telethons, and sang the National Anthems at 2 Stanley Cup Playoffs, and the Edmonton Eskimos Grey Cup playoffs.

During six years as a single mom, I used to listen each day to a radio talk show called "That's Living," with Dr. Henry "Hank" Janzen, Dr. John Paterson, and Dr. Carl Blashko. I learned a lot about healthy living and raising children from listening to their shows, and over the years my favorite was Dr. Janzen. I didn't know what he looked like but thought he must have long white hair and a white beard because he was oh, so wise.

One fall day, as my Klondike Kate jobs were starting to dwindle, I was driving to my agent's office, and wondering what jobs she had lined up for me. I turned on the radio to catch "That's Living," and Dr. Janzen came on the air. He talked about how his wife's battle with liver cancer that had been diagnosed six months earlier, had taken her life. He explained that he needed to share this news that she had passed away with his loyal listeners.

I remember so clearly how he explained why he had to be on the air that day, and how he hoped everyone understood that he needed to work, to take his mind off of his grief, and to help others. He explained how he had been grieving since the day she was diagnosed.

I cried like a baby. I had listened to his updates about her condition for months and felt such a sense of loss and sadness for him. He was kind, and smart and so compassionate and understanding. I remember as I was driving I prayed out loud, "Father, why can't I meet a man like Dr. Janzen, who needs me as much as I need him?"

Not even a month later I got a call from CJCA Radio asking me to host a Fundraiser at the Four Seasons for the Christmas Bureau. We were live on air, and all the celebrities from the station were on the stage with me as I led the carol singing. We raised $10,000 that afternoon.

After the fundraiser, we were all invited to celebrate at the Legion across the street. As I went into the coat room, a man stepped up and helped me put on my coat. This was something new for me! I hadn't met any gentlemen in a long time. As we walked across the street to the Legion, he started speaking, and I recognized his voice. It was Dr. Janzen. He didn't look at all like what I imagined. He was much younger, tall, and good looking. And, he was so sad.

We walked into the Legion, two elderly couples sitting at a table just inside the front door called out to us. He and I both walked over. The men all shook hands, and they said how sad they were to hear about Dr. Janzen's wife. One of the women said to me it was nice to meet me and that I was the best Klondike Kate ever, and that she loved it when I got my young children on stage to sing with me. Then the other woman took my hand, and looked at Hank and said, "You two make such a nice couple! Please take good care of each other."

I had just met him, but at that moment, I looked up into Hank's eyes, and I remembered my prayer. He smiled at me–time stood still, and then we thanked the group and made our way to the CJCA table.

As we sat down with the group, Hank leaned over and asked me for my phone number. I wasn't dating so I gave it to him. Hank called me from Phoenix where he was spending the holidays with his in-laws and his sons.

I t was the first Christmas without their mom. We talked for about fifteen minutes, and then he called me every night at the same time for the next ten days. Our conversations got longer with each phone call, and we talked about our upbringing, our faith, our values, our children, and our hopes and plans for the future. The discussions we had were so honest and so deep that by the time he returned to Edmonton, I felt like we had been dating for a year. We went on our first date to a hockey game, and we were married one year later. I was 33 years old. I learned a valuable lesson: when you pray, be very specific!

As a child, I never experienced a loving family, but today I have that sense of love and security I only dreamed and prayed about. I have learned to love and accept myself, and I am proud of the woman and mother that I have become, despite my past, I have a loving family that is there for me and accepts me for who I am. I have found the security and love in myself, and in my family that keeps growing. Even when we face hardships, as all families do, I never complain because I always remember that I prayed for a large family! I prayed for a secure place where I belonged full of people who loved me! I have all that now–no matter what.

Another way I show myself love is to give myself the affirmations that I longed to hear from others when I was a child and a young adult. You are beautiful. You are worth it. You are enough. You are here for a reason. Your smile makes a difference. You are stronger than you think. You are appreciated. You make a difference. You are loved.

BIO: *Susan Janzen*

Susan Janzen was born in Calgary, and raised in Edmonton, Alberta. As a child, she lived in foster care, in an all-girls convent and off and on with her mother until at age fifteen; she left home to go it alone.

She graduated high school, got married, had two children, and was a professional singer and recording artist for eighteen years. After her divorce in 1982, Susan was honored to represent the City of Edmonton as the first local "Klondike Kate" for two years while raising her two small children. She remarried in 1988, returned to school and graduated with a Bachelor of Education Degree, and taught Special Needs children for six years.

In 2003, she became a licensed Realtor, and today she is a proud mother of five, grandmother of eight, and a great grandma, too! Despite her rough childhood and the challenges she's faced, Susan remains optimistic and full of gratitude.

MaxWell Challenge Realty
780-893-7989
www.susanjanzen.com
Specializing in Accessible and Barrier Free Homes

Epilogue

I sincerely hope that you enjoyed Book 1 in this Breaking the Silence series. Book 1 means that yes, more books will follow. Women and men are already stepping forward to contribute to Book 2, and I invite you to consider if you'd like to be one of them.

If you're feeling called to share your story, please send me a note at
spiritcreek@xplornet.com,
or visit the websites at either: http:://www.sacredheartsrising.com
or http://www.brendahammon.com/sacredheartsrising.html

Regardless of whether you wish to share your story, I hope that what you've read here has touched your heart somehow.

As you immersed yourself in each story, you may have noticed yourself stepping into the shoes of that person, and felt what she was feeling. Empathy is a powerful thing. Reading about the lives of these women here may have reminded you of similar experiences in your life, and you may notice old memories bubbling to the surface. Or perhaps you just enjoyed reading about other women's determination to accept and change their lives.

If old (or recent) memories surfaced and you found this disturbing, I encourage you to seek help in dealing with them. Talk to someone you trust. This could be your doctor, a friend, your minister, or priest. It might mean calling a sexual abuse or domestic violence hotline, seeking spiritual guidance, or searching on the internet for what you need. Above all, please continue asking for help until somebody finally listens to you.

One resource I can offer is the Facebook group "Sacred Hearts Rising." There you'll be able to share your experience in reading the book, as well as your own story, and if you like, to have women who have been there helping you along the way.

As a survivor of multiple traumas, I have used many different modes of therapy, each one helping me in a way that I needed at that time.

Whatever it is, don't be afraid to take that first step. And whatever your journey may be, I wish you the love, success, and healing you need.

Brenda Hammon

Supporters

RuT

©RuT ArT Creations – Biography About the Artist

©RuT ArT portrays intimate portraits of angels that speak, inspire and comfort. The Artist Riette Delport resides in the picturesque town of Mossel Bay about 400 Km to the east of Cape Town, South Africa. Riette draws her inspiration from creating each piece of art from the story of Ruth in the Bible. Ruth was an impeccable woman – loving, kind and full of compassion towards everyone surrounding her. Ruth was loyal and she most of all loved God dearly.

Riette paints some of her art pieces with the absence of facial features hoping that each person would see something of themselves in the piece. It is your interpretation that makes each piece of art unique and personal.

©RuT draws her inspiration from God, Angles, her amazing husband and two wonderful children. She enjoys working with many different types of mediums which included clay, wood portrait and recently she started painting on furniture.

What best describes where she is and what she feels is the following: "Each day we are born again. What we do today is what matters most."

When she is not painting, she spends her time with her family, enjoying reading and playing the cello.

The Facebook page, Rut Artist, mostly included posts of her latest and newest original creations of ©RuT ~ there is also some new creations in different genres that flow out of ©RuT ArT works of art.

Another Facebook page is ©RutCreations ~ this pages includes posts of all the smaller items in die ©Rut brand – creations with images of some of the original artwork is created on products like pendants, gift cards, notepads, brooches, earrings, key rings, and many more.

She also recently started to paint under the alias ©Ruach. The Facebook page is RUACH – the meaning of the word is "Breath of God," under this alias, she will endeavor creations in a multitude of genres…

Look out for her newly updated website www.rutcreations.co, as well the 1st ©Rut Book which project is underway with an invitation to all to participate in the creation journey! Please inbox your email if you are interested in info@rutcreations.co.

A note from the Curator of the artist's work:
"The artist, Riette Delport has been creating these beautiful, fascinating and intricate creations for almost a decade now. Her passion to be creative is reflected on every piece she works on, and the growth in her work is something to behold. She also endeavors to grow into her passion by regularly attending workshops and courses on a personal level to even further enhance this special gift of hers she so humbly shares with us.

An artist that creates paintings like our beloved ©Rut only has so much time on hands. Because of demand, there is always pressure to produce. Her art is not superficial, and a real tangible self-evident investment, the quality, and passion that these original works of art are created with, sets this amazing artist apart from her peers."

Colleen Songs

Colleen Songs is a Canadian Singer-Songwriter who has been spreading her message of using your gifts and talents to lead you to the fulfillment of your wildest dreams.

She began singing and writing when she was 14 and used her talent to take her through adolescence, romance, heartache, back to love, motherhood, wellness, trauma, and the loss of a loved one with mental illness.

She has fought MS for the past 21 years and has recently begun singing once again following a car accident that caused her to have emergency neck surgery, leaving her more afraid of losing her voice than afraid of the surgery.

Currently, Colleen is in the midst of producing her second album, "This Life," with BCCMA and CCMA Award Winning Producer, Tom McKillip. She is publishing her memoir, "INHALE," with Tellwell Publishing Canada, based on the life of a caregiver of a loved one with mental illness, where the gift of song-writing kept the caregiver alive and dreaming her dream.

Her music and speaking journey has brought her as far as Nashville's Canadian Country Music Hall Of Fame, to the stages of eWomen Network, Women Embracing Brilliance, Dreams Take Flight, Kamp Kiwanis, WomenTalk, Blue-Friday, and most recently Gems for Gems, and Sacred Hearts Rising!

With her goal to support anyone's dream of any gender, age, or gift-ability (NOT dis-ability), please welcome Colleen Songs as she inspires the priceless gems within each of us called Gifts and Talents.

And remember..."Dreams Never Expire!" xo Colleen Songs

www.colleensongs.com www.facebook.com/ColleenSongs
www.twitter.com/ColleenSongs
https://www.instagram.com/colleensongsca

Jo Dibblee

Jo Dibblee is determined to be the change she seeks by educating, empowering, and elevating women entrepreneurs via access, connection, collaboration, knowledge, and resources.

She is a Social Entrepreneur who sees it as her responsibility to give back both locally and globally. The founder of Frock Off Inc., Jo is described as a tenacious and fearless philanthropist–a catalyst to change. She works with heart-centered women entrepreneurs who have a big message, product or service that can serve or transform others and are ready to amplify their results.

Jo driven by her passion and purpose which stems from living in hiding for 35 years as a key witness in a murder investigation is committed to global awareness. She has co-hosted a local television show, been a four times international award-winning author, speaker and breakthrough expert. Her award-winning memoir Frock Off: Living Undisguised is the foundation of her work. She has been featured in Canadian media nationwide, and the Huffington Post. Jo is determined to serve 13.1 million women globally.

To learn more and join her community go to www.frockofflive.com

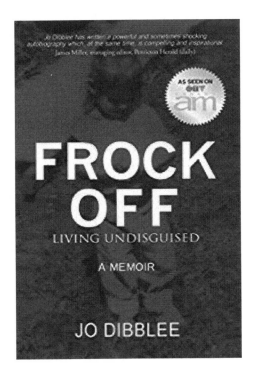

Other books by the author, Brenda Hammon

I Can't Hear the Birds Anymore
by Brenda Portwood

This is a story about sexual, psychological and physical abuse and the ripple effect that this abuse had on my life, and the view I had of myself and the decisions I made during my life as a result of the abuse.

Have to run, have to hide, so alone, so scared…

I can't hear the birds anymore, is a book for all parents, councilors, teachers, etc. who live and work with children. This book shows you firsthand what the abuse feels and looks like through the eyes and the mind of a child.

Hear Me, No Longer Silent

Breaking the Cycle Series Book 1 of 3
International Best Seller

Hear Me is the story of Brenda, a little girl who grew up, learned to listen to herself, and found her true voice.

Hear Me, bears witness to Brenda's isolated struggle with the aftermath of sexual, mental and physical abuse, and how it led her into an abusive marriage and horrific divorce, including a murder contract on her life. By the end of the story, Brenda breaks her silence, and with new confidence, shares her voice.

Most of all this book is about finally saying: Hear Me

Hear Me, the newly revised version of the book, "I can't hear the birds anymore," includes a new introduction by the author and brings fresh focus to her story, revealing the importance of speaking up and helping to break the cycle of abuse.

I AM: Kicking Down the Walls of Silence

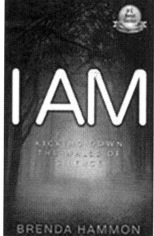

Breaking the Cycle Series Book 2 of 3
International Best Seller and International Award Winner

In these pages, you'll meet two Brenda's. One is a young girl who survives horrific violations and learns to doubt her value, squash her wants, and get caught in a repeating cycle of abuse. The other, an adult woman who gives birth to twin daughters and at that moment, finds a new will to live and to fight for not only her children but for herself. A will, that might be, her only saving grace through the agony of escaping a dark and abusive marriage.

I AM traces the gripping journeys of both Brenda's until, finally, Brenda must decide whether or not she will claim all of herself and step into the fullness of one whole brave, determined woman. This is a story about kicking down those walls, breaking the silence, and reclaiming and rebuilding a life.

This is a story about remembering and recovering the vibrancy of the essential self, the part that cannot be destroyed, and letting that self, light the way forward to healing and wholeness. This is a story that will break your heart and show you not only the way to put it back together again, but also how to see the cracks as portals of light and hope.

Anthologies that Brenda Hammon has contributed to:

In the pages of this book, you will find the stories of 31 amazing women who have the love, the heart, the courage and the wisdom to share their stories with you. While we mention what happened to us, we don't dwell there. We talk about what we have done and what we are currently doing to be well adjusted, happy and productive.

You will find stories from sea to shining sea, and from around the world, and you will discover that the perpetrators of abuse do not respect ethnic, socio-economic, or religious backgrounds.

We share our journeys, the resources and most of all the mindset that we needed to adopt, to achieve the rich and happy lives we are now living.

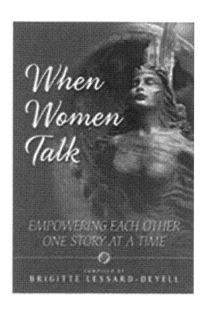

When Women Talk is a collection of stories by women from all walks of life, women who have survived hardship and learned what it means to navigate the world with wisdom, bravery, and balance.

From a once homeless woman to a world traveled financial whiz, from a stay-at-home mother to a postgraduate doctor, the women within these pages demonstrate what it means to stand in your truth and boldly live your best life.

The twin visions behind this anthology are inspiration and engagement. Read it to be inspired by other entrepreneurial women who share experiences that taught valuable business lessons and a successful mindset.

Discover how you can "pay it forward," by using your business success to make positive changes in the world around you.

Let's develop a community of committed women working together to make the world a better place, not just for ourselves but also for future generations.

If you enjoyed this book, please visit Amazon and Goodreads to write a review.

About the Author and Compiler

Inspirational and Motivational Speaker, Entrepreneur, Philanthropist, International Best Selling Author, International Award Winning Writer and equestrian Brenda Hammon kicks down the walls of silence surrounding abuse. Brenda is a catalyst for finding 'Your' happy and has been called an 'Adversity' Expert and has shared her experience on many stages.

Brenda is a storyteller of true life events that everybody is afraid to talk about openly, but want to read about.

Brenda is the CEO and founder of Sacred Hearts Rising.
http://www.sacredheartsrising.com
and also Spirit Creek Publishing, http:// www.spiritcreekpublishing.com.

In denial of the ways abuse had permeated her life for forty years, Brenda suffered in silence and isolation, until finally taking a stand anddealing with her past. Known for her integrity, courage, and directness, Brenda now works to show others who have been abused that they too have a voice and can take back control of their lives. Brenda takes pride in breaking the cycle of abuse in her own family and speaking out loud to prevent the suffering of other children.

Not one to shy away from a challenge, Brenda decided to break the cycle of silence around topics that are not talked about openly in our society.

Also an award-winning rider and trainer, Brenda has competed on the National Circuit in Dressage in Canada. But now with competing behind her, Brenda simply focuses on enjoying and bonding with her horses Hughie and Miss Mini Cooper.

With over two decades of experience in the insurance industry, Brenda and her husband Bud continue to run their own successful insurance business. They also offer training to other independent advisors with Spirit Creek Financial, and their M.G.A. which is designed for independent insurance advisors who are seeking mentoring, guidance, & assistance, being the best that they can be. Brenda also served on the National Advisory Board for one of the leading Lifestyle Protection Companies in Canada's Insurance Industry since the Advisory Boards inception.

Brenda makes her home with her husband Bud on their small farm outside of Alberta Beach, Alberta.

Made in the USA
Columbia, SC
07 August 2018